THE WOODEN SUITCASE

EMMY GOLDACKER

Translated from the German by
H Morgan Waidson and Jean H Waidson

GRENDEL

English translation first published in Great Britain in 2010
by Grendel Publishing

114 Glenarm Road, London E5 0NA

This is a translation of *Der Holzkoffer*, © Adolf Sponholtz Verlag, Inh.
CW Niemeyer Buchverlage GmbH, Hameln

Published with kind permission of Adolf Sponholtz Verlag, Inh.
CW Niemeyer Buchverlage GmbH, Hameln

Translation copyright © H Morgan Waidson and Jean H Waidson

British Library Cataloguing in Publication Data

A CIP catalogue record for this book is available from the British Library

Typeset in Minion Pro

Design by Design@GloryHall.com

Printed and bound in Great Britain by Think Ink, Ipswich

ISBN 978-0-9566570-0-8

INTRODUCTION

Publication History

The Wooden Suitcase first appeared in Paris (*La Valise en Bois,* La Table Ronde, 1976) in Emmy Goldacker's original French (she is married to a French-speaking Swiss, Fred Attinger). Subsequently the version in her original German was published in Hameln in the Federal Republic of Germany (*Der Holzkoffer: Leben und Überleben einer Frau in sowjetischen Lagern,* Sponholtz Verlag, 1982). The English language version (*The Wooden Suitcase,* unpublished MS, 1981) is the work of Jean and Morgan Waidson.

Jean Waidson is the childhood friend mentioned in the last chapter of the book. She and Emmy met at an English/German summer school near Berlin in 1934. They were fifteen and fourteen respectively, became firm friends and, together with their families, had as much contact as possible in the remaining pre-war years. Amongst the published works of Morgan Waidson, formerly Professor of German, Swansea University, are a number of translations mainly from German into English. These include Goethe's *Wilhelm Meister* (6 vols, John Calder, 1977-1982).

Recent second editions of Emmy Goldacker's book are published as *La Valise d'Ivan Ivanovitch,* Éditions Monographic, Switzerland, 2006, and *Ich lebe – genügt das nicht? Ein deutsches Schicksal,* Knaur, 2007. A Russian translation, Деревянный чемодан. Воспоминания узницы советских лагерей, was published by Zvenia (the publishing house of MEMORIAL) under the auspices of the Goethe Institute in Moscow, 2005.

Translators' Introduction

The Wooden Suitcase is an account of the experiences of a German-Jewish woman, Emmy Goldacker, during the most testing and most outwardly adventurous years of her life. As a young woman she was summoned to service with the German Foreign Office in 1941, and it was soon made clear to her that she had no choice but to go where she was sent, mainly in the Balkans. After the collapse of the German resistance to the Allied invasion of 1944-1945, Emmy found herself in Berlin with her mother. Some few weeks of adjustment to post-war conditions saw her teaching with the permission of the authorities in the American Sector. But she was forcibly taken over to the Russian Sector where she was closely confined and subjected to interrogations. This led to her being sentenced to ten years' imprisonment in labour camps in the Arctic Circle. Few German women who also made this journey at the same time as Emmy did survived to tell the tale. It was a desolating experience, lasting from 1945 to 1955, an experience shared not only by other Germans, but by Poles and eventually Russians. The reader travels with Emmy, and even on this terrible journey her essentially cheerful, hopeful nature can find in human contacts consolation and what is almost equanimity, while she can react with vitality and short-term anger to those who would wish to victimize her and to exploit her disadvantaged and precarious position.

When we arrive with Emmy at the labour camp to which she and her fellow prisoners are despatched, we as readers are to follow the narrator in her experience of gruelling physical circumstances and of – at first – unpredictable and bewildering reactions from her captors. Unlikely as it at first seems, we are to get gradually used to the environment of forced labour in Arctic conditions, and to the way in which internees could manage to survive; Emmy Goldacker had youth, vitality and physical strength as well as energy and practical intelligence on her side. The details of camp life, its physical conditions and the various personal relationships that are possible in such circumstances, are presented so soberly and yet also with such imaginative warmth that we as readers are fully caught up in this environment that Emmy evokes, both with humour and emotion, with passion and restraint. Her book is an account of social-historical importance in its objectivity, of emotional impact because of the enormity of the challenges she faced, and of inward depth through the sensitive serenity which the writer can evoke.

This book is a description of a struggle for survival, in itself a grim story. But it is told with such sincerity, humour and grace that far from arousing negative feelings in the reader there remains positive joy at having shared in this affirmation of the invincible nature of the human spirit.

H Morgan and Jean H Waidson

Editors' Introduction

I first met Emmy Goldacker in Berlin in 2003. When she told me about her time in Siberia, she reminded me of my father, who had been a prisoner of war in Java and Sumatra during World War II. Both were extremely grateful to be alive. Neither took anything for granted.

Because she knew how interested I was in her experience, Emmy prepared for me a photocopy of the English translators' typescript. Once I had read her account, I was determined to publish her book in English. Emmy put me in touch with Elspeth, one of the daughters of the translators, and we have worked on it together. Professor Waidson died in 1993 and Mrs Waidson in 1992.

Monica Blake, London 2010

So Why *The Wooden Suitcase?*

The black wooden suitcase given to Emmy by Ivan Ivanovich to carry her possessions to the women's camp in OP turned out to be the only material relic of her ten years in Siberia until, like many other relics, its significance unrecognized, its physical dilapidation all too apparent, it was casually destroyed. Seen only as waste, it was burnt. Now the story is all that remains. The book replaces the suitcase as Emmy's historical record.

That a book should be analogous to a small wooden suitcase (a comparison introduced in the author's preface) seems disarmingly modest – both book and ungainly suitcase being conveyers of 'baggage' – but the analogy is also richly suggestive. Emmy Goldacker's experience and her account of it constantly raise the question of value. A crucifix, which we can assume had spiritual significance for its first owner, a priest, is made of 'heavy gold', facts that impress upon us its monetary value. But exchanged from a cattle truck travelling to Siberia, it is equivalent to only one loaf of bread. The value of the suitcase is equally volatile, ambiguous and suggestive – as by implication is the story, *The Wooden Suitcase.*

Tracing the history of the suitcase backwards, it moves from worthless junk burnt by East German refugees to a black wooden suitcase like everyone else's in Communist Europe, when Emmy finally travels West after her imprisonment. It is a sign merely of the Communist austerity many lived with. When she leaves the Communist Bloc, the suitcase is overflowing with clothes provided by a regime unctuously intent on reconciliation – or is it obliteration of the past? Yet, during her imprisonment, the suitcase and its contents were a treasure, a receptacle for personal property of equally ambiguous value ('my blue and white checked dress with the belt that was so brightly coloured ... my knitting needles ... made out of stiff wire, my toothbrush, found while street-sweeping') and as such symbolic of independent identity, of active endeavour and control, of all that colour represents when one's strictly imposed uniform is black. Such valuation seemed to have been confirmed by its confiscation; it was available only once a year or when Emmy moved camp.

The suitcase also symbolizes a relationship. Ivan Ivanovich, who might have stolen it, has no doubt that it binds him to his 'wife', Shestakova Emma Pavlovna, who will be constantly reminded by the words he inscribes: 'I shall always wait for you'. For him, the suitcase is a symbol of love, protection and possession. Emmy, who does not want to be given his name, sees it differently. It inspires gratitude and even briefly a sense of dependence – a very real need has been met – but within a violent, forced relationship that she looks forward to leaving.

The wooden suitcase as metaphor for Emmy Goldacker's history is powerfully suggestive of all that is difficult, contradictory and impossible to resolve in her experience. And as with the original object, the value of her story can be variously assessed and has been subject to change. The most recent edition of the German version changes the title to a quotation from the last chapter of the book: 'I Am Alive. Isn't That Enough?' followed by a subtitle A German Destiny. Finally Emmy chooses that the life she still has be enough. She rejects revenge, even public judgement for her betrayer as it will merely perpetuate the cycle of violence. Indeed, this urgent generosity is at the heart of the text. Yet, although this is a 'German Destiny' and one which has been documented by Germans other than Emmy, it is also a human destiny. Like many other victims of conflict and dictatorship, identity became a trap for Emmy Goldacker. Potentially vulnerable to Nazi persecution because of her part Jewish origins, she was subsequently identified with those same fascists by the Russians. It is a 'no-win' situation I think many of the powerless would recognize.

Even within her own family, this situation was not unique to Emmy, as she discovered in 1957. Her father, Paul Goldacker, survived his openly Jewish identity by escaping from Nazi Germany in 1938 to settle in Palestine, but he did not survive his German one. In 1940 he died, having been interned as a German by the British. The circumstances of his death remain unclear. (For further information about Paul Goldacker, see 'Geschichte(n) um ein Haus in Dessau-Haideburg' by Peter Löhnert und Emmy Attinger-Goldacker, *Dessauer Kalendar,* 2010, No. 54, pp 70 – 89.)

We, the editors, have, therefore, chosen to use the original title *La Valise en Bois/Der Holzkoffer/The Wooden Suitcase* because of its associations – even for its opacity and awkwardness.

Perhaps the value of the story has fluctuated because it has been vulnerable to assimilation. Of course, it is an autobiography but is it the story of a remarkable woman? A beloved friend? A typical German? A victim of the Cold War? Is it a social and historical record? An account of a spiritual journey? Potential anti-Soviet propaganda? A memorial? It has inevitably been subject to all such interpretations, uses and appropriations since its inception. To its English translators, who knew Emmy, it was important culturally as well as personally. As pacifists, Quakers, and, in my father's case, as an academic, they were acutely aware of war-time and post-war hostility to Germany in Great Britain and were intent on challenging prejudice. They would, I believe, have wanted the English-reading world to relate to Emmy's experience and to her social and moral judgements in such a way that political, nationalist or racist prejudice would be profoundly questioned. My mother also thought the book would make 'a good film'. Whether film informs us of, or glosses over, past sufferings and atrocities is an open question but what is not in doubt is that *The Wooden Suitcase* works as a dramatic – though inevitably distressing – adventure story.

It is hoped that readers of the 21st century, free from the prejudices and censorship of the past century, will value *The Wooden Suitcase* as the gift to the future which it was always intended to be.

Elspeth (Waidson) Knights, London 2010

PREFACE TO THE ENGLISH EDITION

These pages tell a true story, my story, and they include only what I have personally seen and lived through. I have deliberately avoided retelling other people's stories, which are too easily distorted even by their first narrators.

In this, my small wooden suitcase, I bring you the experience of a young woman who was born between two world wars and found out what it meant to live under two dictatorships. (The large suitcase was burned by East German refugees given a home in my mother's house during the early 1960s.) The Nazi administration forced this young woman to work for German counter espionage which became the pretext for Stalin's dictatorship to sentence her to ten years of forced labour.

These words sum up the essence of my experience:

> Wherever I was, I met human beings – whatever the dictatorship they were living under, and these encounters filled me with enormous gratitude. I learned, too, to be grateful for a slice of bread, even if it was black and damp. Such gratitude is a priceless treasure. I want to tell all my readers: life is worth living, whatever the struggle.

Emmy Goldacker, April 2007

To my mother, Johanna Goldacker,
to my husband, Fred,
and to all who, like me, have suffered and hoped.

This English edition is dedicated to my school friend,
Jean McNeille, her husband, Morgan, and her mother,
F M McNeille ('Auntie Peter').

1

Berlin. January 1941

Two SS men guard the front of a big, red-brick building. I hesitate before passing them on my way to the entrance hall.

'How odd!' I think. 'Can this really be a branch of the Foreign Office?'

That was what had been written on the red card I had received a few days before. The card told me my new place of work, and the address on it had been the 'Foreign Office'.

'But why should SS men be on guard here? Perhaps the Foreign Office is being guarded by the SS now. And why not? Nowadays, anything can happen.'

I was afraid and thought of my father who had left Germany in 1938, never to return from his holiday in Italy. I knew that he was in Palestine. And here I was, brought here by the red card – a call to duty which could not be opposed. Should I go in? Should I run away? Where to? Not having the faintest idea, I went past the SS guard and presented my red card at the reception desk. The man behind the glass took it, then examined it carefully. I filled in a form while he made a telephone call. Finally, I was dismissed with, 'Second floor. Room 23. They're expecting you'.

I climbed up to the second floor very, very slowly, wondering what lay ahead, haunted by what lay behind. When I left school in 1938, I had wanted to study languages at the university. That was what was written on my school-leaving certificate anyway. My father, Dr Paul Goldacker, an experimental chemist, had left us years ago, before 1933. He had had an important post in an internationally renowned chemical factory but shortly after I had taken my school-leaving examination, he had left Germany. As he had not responded to his firm's various invitations to return to Germany, he had been dismissed without notice. The house and money intended for my brothers and me were appropriated by the Gestapo. This put an end to all my hopes of studying. I had to earn my living immediately, so instead of attending the university, I took the tram every morning to

Berlin-Lichtenberg. Thanks to my father's professional reputation, remembered even after his escape from Germany, I had been given a post as a secretary with the firm, Aceta, where he had worked. My boss at that time was Dr P Schlack, the inventor of Perlon.

One evening when I had returned home from Lichtenberg to Britz, where I lived with my mother, I had found the red card waiting for me. I was twenty-one years old and I wanted to stay alive. That was why I had come to Berka Street, to this red building, and had not turned away from it. A few days earlier I had lost my elder brother. 'He gave his life for Germany,' just as my younger brother had done in the first week of the war in September 1939.

I wanted to live. I had to stay alive for my mother's sake.

My pace slowed even more once I reached the second floor. Nobody was visible along the entire corridor. Doors were numbered on each side, even ones to the left, odd to the right: 19, 21. I was at number 23. I knocked, a man's voice uttered the routine: 'Come in!' and I entered noticing immediately that this man was not in uniform.

'It is the Foreign Office!' I thought, deeply relieved.

'Miss Goldacker?'

'Yes.'

As this Jewish name was pronounced, I became aware of the portrait of Himmler hanging on the wall behind the man at the desk. I shuddered. When I first went in I had not noticed the picture of this man with his wry mouth and the ice-cold eyes peering through small-lensed spectacles. I no longer know how in spite of my terror I managed, with a pleasant smile, to answer all the questions which were put to me. From behind his desk the official asked the usual questions about my background and my competence in foreign languages, this being the reason I had been summoned. (As a schoolgirl I had spent some time in England and later on had learned Spanish.) In the middle of this exchange the door burst open, a man rushed in, threw his passport on the desk and shouted: 'This is hopeless! How do you think I can go anywhere with this? I might as well put my head in a noose!'

At this point he noticed me and stopped in confusion. I sat still without turning a hair, as though such scenes were commonplace.

The man behind the desk promised him that all necessary steps would be taken to put the matter in order. Almost soundlessly the door was closed.

As I was about to leave, I turned again to the man behind the desk: 'Is there anything else you wish to know about me?'

His answer was lofty, replete with arrogance. 'We can make inquiries without your help, Miss Goldacker!'

I began my new job the next day. My work was to look through Spanish and British newspapers for articles which might be of interest to the State Security Service, Central Office VI, led by Walter Schellenberg. I wrote letters to Spanish agents and translated their reports into German. What had been described on my red card as the 'Foreign Office' turned out to be the headquarters of the German Secret Service. The men working there were nearly all members of the SS, though naturally they were not in uniform. And there was I, with all my fears because of my father, right in the middle of them. However, I soon realized that communication between the Secret Service and the Gestapo was not good and that 'Office VI', where I was working, had no idea of my father's existence in Palestine.

After a few months it was announced that special provisions had been made for conscripts, or people like me who had been directed to work of national importance; those amongst us who were qualified to do so could apply for leave to study, if they wished. This was just what I wanted, so straightaway I took all the necessary steps to be released from the State Security Service. I had managed to save some money, and I was sure that my mother who was now working as a teacher would be able to help me too. What a piece of luck! My study leave was granted. I could already picture myself with my friend, Hartmut, studying at the Berlin Humboldt University. Hartmut had also obtained study leave and would arrive back from the Eastern Front at any moment. Every Sunday he wrote me a long letter which I answered the same day. How wonderful to be alive! Two days later my last letter to Hartmut was returned marked 'Killed in action'. Like me, he was twenty-two years old.

The next day I was called to Walter Schellenberg's office. He and my boss were waiting for me.

2

'How do you like the idea of going to Switzerland? To Lausanne, in fact. You could study there and do a few things for us at the same time.'

The State Security Service would pay for my keep and tuition, and even provide me with pocket money.

'You have twenty-four hours to make up your mind. We should not need to tell you, of course, that this proposition is top security.'

Twenty-four hours in our little house in Britz; twenty-four hours without my being able to confide in a living soul; twenty-four hours I wanted never to come to an end so that I should not have to make this decision. What risk would I be taking if I refused? Obviously they could force me to accept. Perhaps they had known all along that my father was in Palestine. What on earth was I to do? What would happen if I accepted the proposal? There was this 'work' which they had mentioned and which they were naturally not going to tell me about beforehand. But on the other hand, I should be a student; it was true that I knew hardly any French, but that didn't matter. I should be able to leave Germany and live in a neutral country, far away from the war, once more able to walk along lamp-lit streets at night and to see lights in the houses. My mother had left Berlin. Because of the air raids she and her pupils had been evacuated to Slovakia. For what or for whom should I stay in Berlin?

'I accept your proposal,' was my reply after the twenty-four hours had ended.

I was assigned forthwith to the headquarters of the radio section of the State Security Service. I learned Morse and how to manipulate a small transmitter. I was given a camera, a Leica, and was taught how to take and develop photographs of documents. I took part in a course of psychological training, and after I had grasped all these things, almost as though I were playing a game, I was sent to a training centre for spies near Oranienburg. Radio links were maintained here with countries under German occupation, particularly with France, where there was a similar training centre in Paris.

Here, time seemed to stand still. I waited to be called to Lausanne at any moment. But as the days passed, I became more and more oppressed by the obscure and gloomy atmosphere of this training centre. I was not allowed to speak to anyone. The only people I saw were trainees like me as I passed through the garden on my way to the transmitting centre of the school where I worked. Finally something did happen; I was summoned to Wannsee where an SS officer greeted me there with the announcement: 'You go to Istanbul the day after tomorrow!'

'Istanbul?' The word almost stuck in my throat. Slowly I turned round to look at the map hanging on the wall behind and to my left. The rogues! They had promised me Lausanne. I had only accepted the proposal because I wanted to study in Lausanne. What should I do in Istanbul, poised between Europe and Asia and certainly swarming with bugs?

'Are you refusing to go?' My silence was interpreted for me.

The tone of this question brooked no contradiction. I shrugged my shoulders. What else could I do? I was completely in their hands.

I travelled through Slovakia and there said goodbye to my mother who was housed near Bratislava as a teacher under the children's evacuation scheme. When the train started moving slowly out of Bratislava station towards Budapest, my mother stood on the platform, getting smaller and smaller, waving for a very long time. She did not weep. She knew as well as I, the last child remaining to her, that I was not travelling for pleasure. I admired her courage. I was grateful to her for it.

I spent almost twenty-four hours in Sofia, then took the night train to Istanbul which appeared to me the next morning with all its minarets spread out, bathed in a golden light. But the railway station was no different from any other. A tall, fair woman came to meet me. On the way to the hotel she told me that I did not need to be at the Consulate General until four o'clock in the afternoon. Magnificent! I could hardly wait for her to leave me on my own before going out to breathe deeply the air of this free city. I could not resist the temptation to buy a pair of leather sandals (an unaccustomed luxury since the introduction of wooden soles for all German shoes). And then there was the fruit in all the shop windows – raspberries and strawberries, almost the size of little apples – more varieties of vegetables than I had ever seen in my life before and that magnificence of colour, flowers! I had not realized that so much that was beautiful still existed. In Germany there was war, nothing but war, already in its third year. The longer I strolled through this fairytale city, the more Britz, nights of bombing, together with fear and death, became indistinct, seemingly far behind me. Lausanne? Really! Why had I regretted not being sent there? The sun! This city! No, Lausanne could not be any more beautiful.

Punctually at four o'clock I went to the Consulate where I was to work as a secretary. I did indeed write letters there, but I also had to meet with agents. Another reminder of my clandestine role was the transmitter (kept in an office drawer) used to send coded messages to Germany. Agents were usually to be met in some café or other. One day I was supposed to meet a Greek. I arrived earlier than agreed and sat down at a table at the Park Hotel, close to the Consulate. The man whom I was to meet, seeming to recognize me, came up to me without hesitation. As he greeted me he slipped an unusually large diamond ring into my hand. I understood instinctively that he wanted to put me under an obligation to pass information to him directly. That I did not want. Still smiling, I folded up my newspaper, inserted the ring unobtrusively into it and using this, returned his present to him. He was obviously very annoyed.

'I give presents to all Consulate staff with whom I have dealings,' he said crossly, 'You are the first to refuse.'

'I daresay, like them, I would have accepted some small gift, but not such a valuable one as this.'

He passed on the information which I was due to collect, turned away and left, obviously put out.

I told my boss about this incident at once! 'The Greek!' he said. 'But, Miss Goldacker, we've been dealing with him for months, and he hasn't given us the slightest reason to doubt his loyalty – to us. What is more, he's married to a German. Your overhasty warning is completely superfluous!' How I detested his unpleasant, arrogant tone of voice!

A few days later, I attended a small party given by the Greek. Very many of the guests were strangers to me. For the first time in my life I ate goat's milk cheese and black olives and drank raki. What a treat! After a while the Greek took me to a nearby room, and opened the drawer of a chest; it was filled to the brim with gold bars.

'Please, help yourself.'

'I wouldn't know what to do with them,' I replied and left him alone with his treasures.

This time naturally, I refrained from saying anything at all about it at the Consulate. One overbearing, arrogant reply had been enough. It was not very long, only a few days, before the Consulate had the unpleasant surprise of seeing the Greek, whom they had regarded as so trustworthy, in the company of the Americans. Of course he had been passing on all he knew about German counter-espionage in Istanbul to them, and the information must certainly have earned him further gold bars.

One morning, when I left the guesthouse where I was living, stepping cheerfully into the early sunlight, I bumped into a man whom I had already seen a few times at the Consulate. He seemed to be going the same way as I was, so we walked together, laughing and talking. What a magnificent morning! When I finally arrived at my office door, I caught myself smiling and whistling to myself. And when I came back again to my guesthouse in the evening, I found a letter waiting for me signed by the Rumanian military attaché. He wanted to see me again.

I was very happy, for I also wanted us to meet again. But then, once again, I felt the familiar fear – my father was in Palestine; I was called up for service with German counter-espionage led by the SS; my mother was with her class of children in territory under German occupation. The slightest carelessness on my part could have the worst possible consequences for me and my mother. Yet I really did want to see this military attaché again!

The next morning I told my boss about his letter. 'Serge Ulescu? One of our best agents. He has connections in important political circles in Turkey. As a Rumanian officer he believes that he is working for the German military intelligence service[1] and has no idea that he has put his services at the disposal of us, the State Security Service. On no

[1] At that time still under the supreme direction of Wilhelm Canaris.

account must we lose him. I advise you, therefore, to hint cautiously to him that you are, hm, shall we say engaged and are unwilling to enter into any sort of relationship here. However, I am drawing your attention to the fact that the State Security Service cannot afford to lose its best agent. So be careful, please!'

I wanted to be careful and thought that it would be best to meet Serge just one more time, just long enough to tell him personally and in a very friendly manner – this sort of thing is easier to say in a friendly manner than to write, I thought – well, to tell him what? Certainly, my boss was right; I should tell him that I was engaged and didn't want to become involved with anyone here in Istanbul. He must and he would understand that; certainly, this explanation could not offend him.

On the evening when we had arranged to meet, I had endless trouble decoding a message from Wannsee (radio messages were usually transmitted in the evening or at night because then the reception was better). I was over an hour late when I finally arrived at what I believed would be our only rendezvous and Serge was still waiting for me. He greeted me so warmly, in spite of the long wait; he seemed to be so happy that I simply could not bring myself to make my thoroughly prepared, little speech. 'Later', I thought, 'at the end of the evening, perhaps another time.'

I never delivered that speech.

We saw each other more and more frequently. I was in love with him although – or because – he could have been my father. We took all possible precautions to avoid being seen together. Agent Number 7075, as before, brought important information to Consul D. Consul D had no idea that I had not followed his good advice until the day the Turkish police intervened.

The police had long suspected that Serge was working for the Germans but they, having no proof, were unable to expel him or indeed even to arrest him. Of course, Serge had a diplomatic passport; of course, I did not. Consequently it would be easy to put pressure on him through me. On one particularly lovely summer morning, Consul D burst into my office, pale with anger.

'I knew this would happen. What a mess! When I remember how

I advised you – caring for you like a father – not to enter into this relationship. But, oh no, Miss Goldacker always knows best and just does what she wants. And now we're for it!' He wildly waved a piece of paper which I took to be a photocopy.

'Do you know what I've got here?' he shouted.

How was I to know?

'A warrant for your arrest! The Turkish police are already waiting for you!'

He was in such a rage that his only ambition, it seemed, was to throttle me. Quite calmly, I said, 'What do you want me to say? Let the Turkish police arrest me! I don't know anything about Serge Ulescu's activity. Mr D, it was you who dealt with him, not me. I love him, that is all there is to it.'

'You told him, of course, that he's working for us, didn't you?'

'No, we had more important things to say to each other.'

'Be quiet, will you?' he shouted at me.

At that time Germany was in such a precarious position – the great retreat after the defeat at Stalingrad had begun – that a German agency abroad simply could not afford to allow a consular employee to be arrested in what had been until then a neutral country.

'You must stay here in this room. No telephone calls. This is an order now, not advice. The train to Sofia leaves shortly before four o'clock, and you are taking it; you will go under escort so that we can be sure that you really do arrive in Sofia. Is that clear?'

It was! Towards midday, when all the other consular employees had gone to lunch and I was completely on my own in the office, I took the telephone receiver off the hook. When I started to dial Serge's number there was a suspicious choking noise. I put the receiver down.

Later, when I was given my passport for the journey, I immediately saw that it was not made out in my name. I could not help remembering my first day at the head office of the State Security Service: 'How do you think I can go anywhere with this? I might as well put my head in a noose!' Now it was my turn.

We (my 'guard' and I) came to the station without any mishap – as might be expected in a car provided with a large 'CD'. As if by chance, the German ambassador, von Papen, had just arrived from

Ankara and was walking up and down in front of the station building. Whether it really was by chance, or whether it was a precaution, to enable immediate action if I were arrested, I still do not know.

When I had to show my passport at Edirne, the station at the Turkish-Bulgarian frontier, I took a cigarette from my handbag.

'Have you a light, please?'

Of course the customs official had a light and he did not look at my forged passport. After the passport formalities were over and we had arrived safely on Bulgarian territory, my companion breathed an audible sigh of relief. Later in Sofia he confessed to me that he had admired my calm. He claimed he had been quaking with fear.

Two long weeks of waiting in Sofia followed, two weeks that seemed endless, and during which I hoped and expected that Serge would get me out; meanwhile the head office of the State Security Service was in no rush to give me instructions. Evening after evening I went to the station and waited for the train from Istanbul.

Eventually I was summoned back to Berlin, and there the Gestapo interrogations started. They assumed that I had told Serge for whom he was really working. I kept on repeating the same thing, exactly what I had said to Consul D in Istanbul. That is, that in our conversations, there had been no mention of Canaris, let alone of Kaltenbrunner[2] or Schellenberg. We had other things to talk about. During one cross-examination I was ordered to produce immediately any letters or other news that I might have received from Turkey and to hand them over to the Gestapo officer who was interrogating me.

Every evening from that day on I barricaded myself inside our house in Britz. I knew that they often came in the night so I heaped up several chairs on top of one another behind the front door. The clatter of the falling chairs would wake me if they did try to fetch me at night. Three weeks passed; during the day there were interrogations, at night I was in an agony of fear. When I came back to Britz one day after a cross-examination, I found a long telegram from Serge in the letterbox. Serge! Serge! If you only knew! He wrote that he did not believe any of the things he had been told about me. What had they been saying about me? He also said he looked forward to our meeting again soon.

---

[2] The Austrian Ernst Kaltenbrunner was Head of the State Security Office (RSHA, Reichssicherheitshauptamtes).

Could it be possible? He wrote about meeting again. I re-read the telegram until I knew it by heart. What had they told Serge about me? Was the whole thing a trap to find out whether I would take the telegram to the Gestapo? I was on my own and had time to think things out. No, I was not going to hand over the telegram; nobody could prove that I had received it. I had not signed anything, so I had not received anything either. I kept on saying to myself aloud, 'I haven't signed anything, so I haven't received anything either.'

Then the telephone rang. The Gestapo! I always had to be available, except when I was on my way from home to the Gestapo and back. Of course, they had known about the telegram a long time, I panicked. But it was my Austrian friend who was on the line, not the Gestapo. I was to go to the head office of the State Security Service straight away.

'Bad news?' I asked briefly.

'No, no. The opposite. Just hurry along here.'

Relieved, I once more read through the telegram, which I already knew by heart, before burning it. 'A telegram? No, I haven't had a telegram.'

At the head office of the State Security Service, I was received so cordially that I straightaway sensed that I had some power. The much-too-friendly smile and the voice of the man opposite me led me to guess right away that I was going to be asked a favour.

'Could you please write a few lines to 7075 so that he knows that you are all right? But please tell him at the same time that you have met your fiancé again and that he must not cherish vain hopes.'

'I shall be glad to write that I am well, but anything else – oh no!'

'Very well then. The main thing is for you to write to him in a friendly way; though of course, not too friendly; 7075 must be reassured that things are going well with you, that you are alive.'

So that was it! I wrote a short and completely insignificant letter. Right at the end, at the bottom on the left, I wrote 'Norok', the only Rumanian word that I knew. We had often said it to one another. It means 'good luck'.

'What's this supposed to be down here, this "Norok"?' the SS officer asked, in a rather less friendly tone when he read through the letter.

'Nothing special. We would say, "Cheers!"'

He took my letter and sent it off at once. When I left his office I passed a half-open door. My Austrian friend pulled me inside, and whispered to me: '7075 has refused to work for us any more unless he receives a letter in your handwriting by tomorrow evening. They've told him impossible stories about you. He believed them at first, but then the lies became so blatant he realized that the whole thing was made up. Since then he has been afraid for your liberty, even your life, and has stopped bringing any further information. They've got themselves into a real mess.'

The following December I saw Serge again in Vienna. He came via Sofia which at that time was occupied by the Germans, and was where he had handed over a parcel to one of the State Security Service men. In return for doing this, he had received a German passport in the name of 'Ludwig Specht', which meant he could see me in Vienna without his own Rumanian passport being stamped. How stupid to give him the name, 'Ludwig Specht'; his handkerchiefs and shirts had all been marked clearly and in large letters with his monogram 'SU'.

We became engaged at a ceremony in the Cathedral of St Stephan. Before the altar of the Virgin Mary he placed a platinum ring on my left ring finger. He had had his full name and a date (10.7.1942) engraved on it. Later on he gave me two French gold coins.

'Perhaps you will need them one day. But be careful, don't let anybody see them. You could get into trouble again if you had to explain how you got them.'

Fear once more; my smile froze. The future lay in front of me like a long, dark tunnel with no hint of any light at the end.

'Come, Serge, let's have some tea.'

We drank champagne out of teacups, in a hotel in Vienna. It was the fourth year of the war. Of course, the State Security Service did not give us permission to marry. Serge had to return to Istanbul alone. And he had to continue working for the State Security Service, if he wanted me to remain unharmed in Berlin.

3

Every day bombing attacks on Berlin grew worse. Whenever I was summoned to the head office of the State Security Service, I could hardly bear the hypocritical friendliness with which I was treated. I had not forgotten the Gestapo interrogations, nor the fear that had tormented me for three weeks at home in Britz: 'Will they come tonight and fetch me?'

'Will you work for us at the Japanese General Consulate in Vienna?'

'In Vienna? Why not? What am I to do there?'

'The Japanese General Consul is looking for a secretary who is to listen on his behalf to the British news and to translate it. We don't like the Consul's attitude, and we should like to know more about him and the company he keeps. I take it that I don't need to tell you that you haven't been sent there by us, of course. Tell him anything you like.'

So I went to Vienna again, as an unattached student who had lost everything in an air raid; with no papers and no testimonials, nothing but my overcoat and my life. The Consul believed every word of my story and made no difficulties about employing me. I did not send a single memorandum about him to Berlin. I listened in to British news bulletins when the fancy took me; when I was not in the mood I simply took a large piece of white paper and wrote on it, 'Completely incomprehensible. German interference.'

Meanwhile my Austrian friends had also returned to Vienna. I lived with them and so did not need to accept the Japanese Consul's offer of the elegant flat next to my office in the Consulate. Even so, the grand piano there took my fancy; because it was so close to my office, it had to suffer my poor versions of Chopin or Mozart. I regularly had letters from Serge, sometimes even parcels, sent to me via the Berlin office. Serge and I still hoped to meet. By and large my time working at the Japanese General Consulate was happy. Vienna in spring-time was as lovely as it always had been, in spite of this being the fifth year of the war. The war went on – but I had no one to lose any more. Nobody. They were all dead – my brothers, my cousins, my friends. They all died for 'Great Germany'.

But I loved Serge. I loved life. Serge.

On 29 April, the Japanese colony in Vienna was invited to a big celebration at the Consulate; it was the Emperor's birthday. I too was among the guests! What an honour! The evening beforehand a Japanese consular official initiated me into the secrets of this festivity, so that I would be able to follow established procedure; bow before the gigantic oil paintings of Tenno and his spouse, then withdraw again, keeping my eyes fixed upon the two portraits. These two pictures hung in the small drawing room on the wall facing the door. I stood amongst all the Japanese in the big entrance hall of the Consulate waiting my turn, being the last person to bow with my arms folded over my chest before their Majesties in oil. I cannot imagine how I managed to stop myself laughing out loud as I walked backwards to join the group of Japanese who had already paid their respects to their Emperor and God; but I succeeded in keeping my eyes rigidly fixed on the oil painting of the reigning couple, as I had been taught during the previous evening. After this, we stood in a corner of the drawing room and waited for a formal address from the General Consul.

He came, small and rotund, a broad, brightly-coloured sash wound about his tight-fitting evening dress in honour of the occasion. He looked so funny that I did not dare to look at him while he spoke. I did not understand a word of Japanese, and it was so strange to me to hear this unfamiliar language spoken by the small, rotund man with the sash that I turned away to conceal my laughter. But who did I see in the mirror? Me, giggling, hopelessly failing to be suitably serious. The servant rescued me from my silly mood when he entered carrying a tray of glasses filled with champagne. We all drank the health of the Japanese emperor.

Before I went to this gathering, one of my Austrian friends had joked, 'Bring something back for us. There should be something good in the Consulate'. (It was the fifth year of the war. Food was short.)

'Of course, I'll bring you something back.'

I kept my promise and arranged for small pastries, slices of glazed duck, cigarettes, large pieces of cream cake and small sandwiches to disappear into my large, lizard-skin handbag. It was quite easy; I needed only to stroll slowly and inconspicuously past the many richly laden tables, big and small.

A young Consulate employee, Otto Hahn, took almost as much interest as the Consul himself in the British news bulletins which I translated. As the son of a Jewish father and a Japanese mother he was happy to have found some sort of refuge in the Japanese Consulate. There he was occupied with routine office duties such as putting out letters and documents, so he was able to read my translations before he laid them out. The head office of the State Security Service seemed to have forgotten me; they had other things to worry about for sure, and the private life of Consul Y no longer interested them.

When the Americans began to bomb Vienna, the Japanese Consul was dreadfully afraid. However, the raids were nothing compared to those I had experienced in Berlin. These first raids mainly involved reconnaissance flights, but as soon as the air-raid warning sounded, the Consul put on a steel helmet, clamped a bottle of whisky under his arm, and took first place in the lift down to the cellar. When he thought he had time, he told his chauffeur to drive him quickly to the Imperial Hotel, where the cellar was deeper and safer.

After some months, they suddenly remembered me in Berlin and ordered me to go to Zossen, near Berlin, where part of the senior staff of the State Security Service had been evacuated. There I was told personally, 'Serge Ulescu insists on your going to Istanbul. In consideration of the services rendered by him hitherto and in order to place him under obligation to us in the future, we consider ourselves compelled to comply with his request and to send you to Istanbul. However, if diplomatic relations should be broken off between Germany and Turkey,' the SS officer continued, 'you are to report at once to the German General Consulate, in order to wait there for your repatriation to Germany. Do you understand?'

'Yes, of course.'

I was to fly from Vienna to Istanbul by the next courier plane. I could not conceal my happiness at this news. The SS officer went on, 'If I am correctly informed, you still have brothers, haven't you, Miss Goldacker? I mention this in case you should prefer to stay in Turkey.'

'My brothers and my cousins are all dead. They died for Great Germany.'

I could not help these words; hatred and contempt could be

discerned in my voice.

'And your mother?'

'I understand. I shall come back.'

Once in Vienna again, I had just three days to prepare for my flight to Istanbul. First, there was the Japanese Consul, whose employment I had to leave at once. How could I best organise this? What sort of a reason should I give him? I had a brilliant idea; the Consul had often invited me in the past to listen to the British news in the evening or even at night in his flat instead of in the office. I was young and people often said to me that I was quite pretty. Why shouldn't I make the most of this for once? I could lead him on and when he 'lost control', I would be offended and run away. It was not at all difficult; we both sat in the large dining room, and everything went as planned; I rushed out of the Consulate, crying out noisily.

In just two days I should be flying to Istanbul. Just two more days. The next day my passport would surely arrive from Berlin; the day after that I should be flying with the courier plane to Istanbul. My mother came from Poland, where she had been with evacuated children, and we stayed with Austrian relatives. She had come to say goodbye to me for a second time, this time probably for ever. She concealed her sadness so bravely; I was ashamed to be so full of happiness. The next morning a surprise visitor arrived – the Consul himself, who had come to apologize to me formally for his behaviour of the previous evening and to request that I resume my work in the Consulate. I accepted all his apologies, but did not return to the Consulate.

By the evening my passport should have arrived from Berlin, but it did not come. I did have a passport, it was true, but as it was made out in my own name I could not enter Turkey with it, for there was every chance that I was still on their list of wanted persons. The next day the courier plane flew to Istanbul without me.

'I shall just have to fly next Tuesday,' I said disappointedly to my friends.

One week after another passed; my passport did not come, and the courier plane from Vienna to Istanbul flew Tuesday after Tuesday without me. After some weeks I received a message from Berlin; I was to be patient. The delay in my departure was to be ascribed to the momentarily prevailing tension in German-Turkish relations. 'A pack of lies,' I thought, but a short time later diplomatic relations between Turkey and Germany were broken off, as head office had rightly anticipated. I was left in peace; no one troubled about me any more. But I understood that I should never travel to Istanbul again.

Serge – how should it be otherwise? – of course, continued to send important information to the State Security Service. He continued even after the Germans had left Istanbul. Sometimes his messages consisted solely of greetings to me. I received his last greeting from the transmission centre in Berlin-Wannsee shortly before the end of the war, in February 1945.

In the midst of war, in September 1944, I could travel freely and without anxiety between Vienna and Prague. My mother was now near Prague, still with evacuated children. But it was impossible for me to go back to the Japanese Consulate after my 'flight'. What about money? That was no problem; Berlin remitted my salary regularly to Vienna, without otherwise remembering anything about me. Where could I set off for now? My mother in Prague? No, I did not feel at all drawn to this idea. Perhaps to my sister-in-law who was living at that time with her two small children in the Bohemian Forest? I made up my mind to go there and was about to go to the Vienna West Station to inquire about train connections, when the doorbell rang. 'It must be our neighbour for his newspapers,' I thought and opened the flat door.

'Does Miss Goldacker still live here?' the man asked.

'Yes, here I am. What do you want?'

He turned back the left lapel of his jacket and I saw the Gestapo badge.

'Gestapo! Follow me. You are under arrest.'

'Will you please allow me to get changed?' I asked, and pointed to my lightweight grey silk dress.

He gave his permission. Once in my room I hurriedly wrote a few explanatory and soothing words to my friends and left my ration card for them. They would have greater need of it than I would in the place where I was now being taken. In spite of the warm summer weather I put on a suit and a thick pullover – Gestapo cellars were bound to be cold. I stuffed some underwear and my toothbrush into my handbag and did not leap down from the balcony, as I had done in a recent dream. I had anticipated arrest in that dream. 'Let's wait – for the time being,' I said to myself. I had to go on living, for my mother's sake, for myself, for Serge. The man was waiting outside in the corridor. We went down the four storeys together, into the street and along the Liniengasse, side by side, like a pair of lovers who had had a quarrel.

While we were walking silently in the direction of the Margarethengürtel, I feverishly considered what might be the reason for my arrest. Serge? Was he no longer willing to work for Germany? My father? One day it was bound to come out that he was in Palestine! Who else? Perhaps somebody who was witness to a conversation in which I spoke about the British news bulletins that I had heard? After all, recently there had been that stranger at my cousin's house at Kaasgrabengasse 69. My cousin and his wife knew very well where I was working. I had often told them about what I had been listening to. I had nothing to fear from them but what about that stranger whose name I could not even remember any more?

'Do you know Otto Hahn?'

This put an end to all my speculations.

'Of course I do.'

'Do you also know that he has already had a month in a concentration camp because of you?'

'Because of me?'

I was extremely sorry for the young man, but at the same time I breathed a sigh of relief. So that was it! I positively frisked through the last part of my journey to the City Railway. When we arrived, my companion, showing his season ticket, passed straight through the barrier, without concerning himself about me. I was left standing. They arrested me and then expected me to pay my own rail fare! Once he had reached the platform below, the man turned back to me, saying, 'What's the matter? Are you coming, or have I got to fetch you?'

'Will you buy my ticket please?' I asked in a very friendly voice.

He came up the steps again and bought my ticket but not in a friendly way at all. We stayed silent in the City Railway, got out at the Schwedenplatz and made our way to the big Gestapo building. There it was again, this feeling of fear. At the entrance I was supposed to fill in a form as a visitor, just as I had done previously in Berka Street. As I looked in my bag among underclothes, toothbrush and other things for my identity card which was valid in Vienna as well as in Berlin, my companion stared at me speechlessly and eventually stuttered out, 'Why didn't you tell me right away who sent you to the Japanese Consulate?'

'Did you ever ask me? It was certainly not my business to give you any explanation without being invited to.'

'Did you know that we've been trying to find you in Berlin and Prague? We've been looking for you for ages, but today it came to me that you still might be in Vienna. And there you were at the Japanese General Consulate on the instructions of the State Security Service!'

In spite of this explanation I had to accompany him to the fourth floor, where there were a few offices and many cells. We went through an iron trellis door which closed automatically behind us. I cast a glance out of the window. The summer sun shone down. Was I seeing it for the last time?

Everything became clear in the interrogating officer's room; Otto Hahn's task in the Japanese Consulate was to classify and to file papers. While doing this, he saw the translations of the British news bulletins every day, and he just devoured them. He had been talking about them – it was not my fault. If only I could have helped him in some way! After I returned to my relatives in the Liniengasse I spent the whole evening trembling like an aspen leaf.

The war still went on. Eventually I went back to Berlin, although my relatives advised me against it; but I wanted to go home! In Berlin things were chaotic; employees of the State Security Service and of other official organizations were burning lists and files; no one worked any longer; their sole occupation at that point was to destroy things. Everybody was trying to rescue what they could of their personal possessions. Every night the air-raid sirens went three or four times. I had had enough of always going into the air-raid shelter. 'If I am to die now, I can die just as well in bed,' I said to myself, and the next time there was an air-raid warning I pulled the bedcovers over my head.

'It's more comfortable to die like this,' I decided. The coverlet bears the traces of my heroism even to this day; innumerable splinters of glass from shattered window panes slashed it to pieces. The next morning I nailed the windows up with cardboard and stayed in my bed again.

One day the war really was over. Berlin burned, and the sun failed to penetrate the thick banks of smoke which lay over the whole city. The sudden quiet was uncanny and terrifying. No further bomb attacks, no Russian tanks going along the roads, and crossing diagonally through our little gardens. Our house in Britz was almost completely destroyed by bombing but shortly before the end of the war my mother appeared in Berlin again.

When at last the sun could shine down on this apocalyptic scene, the man appeared for the first time at our house. He was a former concentration camp prisoner, had only one arm, and after his liberation was working for the Russians.

'I am supposed to search the premises here,' he said, almost embarrassed in his manner.

'Please do. You will be lucky if you find anything incriminating here. I have never had anything like that at home. I was too unimportant for that. Anyway, don't you realise that I'd have had plenty of time to burn everything?'

'You may well be right,' he said and left.

A few days later, however, he came back.

'This time I am to arrest you!'

I could feel myself turning pale. He looked first at me and then at my mother. Then he noticed the photographs of my brothers which had been framed with a small quantity of mourning crepe. He looked once more at my mother who was sitting there motionless.

'Perhaps you were not at home, do you think? That is – after all – quite likely.'

And he went off again without a sound.

I had acquired some veronal from a friend. At first Berlin had been occupied only by the Russians, the Allies having halted at the River Elbe. I had no idea how and where I should take flight. I might have managed on my own – I was young – but what would happen to my elderly mother? I brought two glasses and some water into the dining room and put out enough veronal to end our lives. We looked at each other.

'You see, Mummy, Wolfgang and Guntram have gone on ahead of us. You needn't be afraid.'

'Stop it! You mustn't do it!' shouted Ingrid, our neighbour's grown-up daughter, who had come up into our house through the cellar bringing us a few sandwiches – a treat in those times!

Today I realize that she was right. First we had to wait and see. Our district would soon be under American control, and then everything would certainly look different. I was almost ashamed of my cowardice.

Life slowly began to return to normal. Some of the first institutions to be revived directly after the war's end were schools. Teachers were needed everywhere. Any teachers who had been in the Nazi Party were dismissed – and nearly all teachers had been in the Party! However, my mother who had, of course, never been a Party member could start teaching again at once. Crash courses were set up for girls who were about to qualify at eighteen (who likewise had not been Party members), to train them to be teachers and so to overcome the shortage. Part of the training course consisted of observing lessons given by qualified teachers. I trained at my mother's school, as a matter of course. One morning there was a knock at the classroom door. 'Is Miss Goldacker there?'

'Yes, here I am.'

'Please come along with me!'

It was a man, like the one in Vienna who had invited me to go with him to the Gestapo only this time he came from the NKVD[3]. Once again, I was wearing my grey silk dress. This time, I was quite sure that there must be a mistake, and that I should be back home again in the evening. When the man, a German, brought me to the Russians, he was not in the least embarrassed to receive a packet of cigarettes and a bottle of vodka in my presence as payment so to speak.

The Russians to whom I was taken were installed in a bomb-damaged school. I was locked in the cellar which was still almost intact, and at dusk two Russian soldiers brought me on foot through the ruins of

[3] People's Commissariat for Internal Affairs.

Berlin to Treptow. On the way I dropped my passport into a street drain without being noticed. After walking for about two hours we stopped in front of a detached house in its own grounds. As this house showed no obvious signs of bomb damage, it had, of course, been requisitioned by the Russians. What a strange coincidence! Years ago as a child I had played with the children of the house, and I recognized it all again – the gravel-strewn courtyard, the long corridor, and further on, the highly polished parquet flooring in the many rooms.

'Sit down there!' one of the two men said to me and pointed to a bench.

I sat down near an old man who was huddled up, waiting there. He caught sight of my wristwatch, and muttered between his teeth: 'Hide your watch and anything else you value. In there' – and he pointed with his head to the door opposite – 'you will be searched straightaway and absolutely everything will be taken away from you!'

I thanked him with a smile. Although it was summer I had put on my boots – it had been raining in the morning – and my light grey summer coat. Then I thought of an old saying: 'left is lucky', and slipped the watch into my left boot, along with my engagement ring, the two gold coins Serge had given me in Vienna and my compact containing the veronal (I was still ready for all eventualities).

The door opposite was already being opened, and I was told to go in. One of the three men present in the room immediately snatched my handbag from me and rummaged around in it. The second man took my coat.

'Sit down,' the third man indicated.

I took the only chair in the room.

'Shoes off!' he snapped at me.

Slow and leisurely, I took off my right boot. The soldier seized hold of it, turned it upside down and searched vainly on the floor for any thing that might have fallen out. Then he returned it. I put it on again, laughing. He asked me for the other boot – and nothing venture, nothing gain – I gave him the same boot a second time. He did not notice.

I was taken down into the coal cellar where there were already two figures crouching on empty sacks – a very young man who was tormented by epileptic fits, and a young and very beautiful woman. She was an actress, and with her beautifully modulated voice she recited long speeches from Lessing's Minna von Barnhelm. I had once learnt the part of the lady's maid, and so I could reply to her. Our meals – we were given them every other day – consisted of a bowl of lukewarm water with a few cabbage leaves swimming around in it. Now and again we were taken to the upper floors of the house to be interrogated, and we invariably had to cross through a large room where there was always (or so it seemed to me) a cold buffet ready which our guards proceeded to enjoy in our presence. After this, they loudly and uninhibitedly smacked their lips and led us on further through the house.

One night when I had just gone to sleep on my coal sack, someone came to fetch me. While I was still half asleep, I found myself suddenly seated in the middle of a room, dazzled by two floodlights that were directed at me. Facing me on the other side of the room I could obscurely make out the shadowy figures of three or four men. They at once started to bombard me with questions.

'Who was your controller?'

'What are the names of the other agents? Who was responsible for the accident in Sofia? Where were you in July 1942? What is the name of the agent who set up the bogus spy ring in Sofia? If you answer, you'll be set free!'

'I don't know anybody. Only numbers. You should know this better than I do; agents never know each other.' I said all this very softly, without the slightest fear, and without realizing that I had not removed my engagement ring which up till now I had always put in my mouth during interrogations – I had had rehearsals down in the cellar, and had found out that I could speak very well with the ring in my mouth. I only needed to fix it in between a wisdom tooth and cheek. This ring contained the answer to very many of the questions put to me; on it there was the full name of Serge, who in the meantime was being sought by the Russians and the Americans, as well as a date which also threw light on a good number of questions. Only when I was aware of the fixed stare of an officer directed at my hands on my knees, did I think, 'My ring!' Then it was all I could think of. Now everything was lost and my fibs were pointless. For it had been Serge who had brought the transmitter in December 1943 to Sofia where he had been supposed to be setting up a spy ring for the Americans. Ostensibly he had been working for the Americans but he passed on the Allies' transmitter and code to a man from the State Security Service. And the time that he would have needed for setting up the spy ring had been spent with me in Vienna, under the pseudonym, Ludwig Specht. His Rumanian passport contained no entries relating to this. 'Hopeless,' I thought and let the ring slip into my hand ready to give it to the officer who was coming towards me. I was paralyzed with fear. The officer's voice seemed distant, as if blocked by a thick mist: 'Aren't you ashamed to be sitting here in front of us with coal-black fingernails?'

Suddenly liberated from this torturing fear, I shouted back angrily: 'Why should I be ashamed? That's too much! You keep me for a fortnight in a coal cellar, and then you expect me to have clean fingernails. I don't even get drinking water, only wretched watery soup every other day.'

There followed a deathly silence, then the interrogation continued quietly.

One night I was taken to a room containing a very long table; at one end sat the examining magistrate, I had to sit at the other. Between us, approximately halfway down one long side, sat the interpreter. Just in front of the officer was a bundle wrapped in a scarf, the scarf I wore when I was arrested. A corner of my bag was visible and protruding out of the bundle were photographs of Serge. One had been taken in Bucharest, another in Istanbul, and a third in Vienna, in front of the Charles Church. Each of these photographs had a stamp on the back which indicated the place and date of the snapshot. The officer's pistol was lying to the right of the bundle, and a rubber truncheon was near to it on the left.

The interrogation took its usual course; I was continually asked for the names of colleagues and agents.

'I don't know any names! You can have as many numbers from me as you like!'

The interrogation became protracted. At one point, the interpreter, visibly struggling not to fall asleep, went out. Things were not much better for the officer; he nodded off while the interpreter was out of the room. Only I was wide awake, waiting fearfully for the bundle with the photographs to be opened.

I had to do something. I carefully advised myself, 'Everything that you do now, you must do quite slowly. There must be no hasty, sudden movements.' That after all was what I had been taught. I got up slowly and crept silently and cautiously along the endlessly long table until I reached the bundle; I undid the knot, took the bag in my hand and slipped the pictures of Serge into my left boot. Then I crept back again just as slowly and quietly, keeping my eyes on the sleeping officer and the bundle in front of him. I had hardly regained my seat when the door opened and the officer, woken up by the noise, gave a start. When the interpreter sat down again, I asked to go to the toilet, which was permitted. Here I cast a last look at Serge's picture then flushed away the torn-up scraps of the photos. When I came back, I saw the officer had opened the bundle.

'Who is that?' the officer asked me and pointed to a picture of my mother.

'My mother.'

'And who is this?'

'One of my brothers.'

My whole family suddenly came to life before me, on that long table, between truncheon and revolver.

Once I was back in my coal cellar, I felt assured that they would let me go soon. For, what had they actually got against me? One morning about three weeks later two guards came telling me, 'Put your things together. You are going home!'

I believed them. And why not? I was radiant as I took my leave from my fellow prisoners and went up the cellar steps between the guards. Outside, in front of the garden gate, was a lorry with armed soldiers and prisoners on it.

'Up you get,' one of my guards said grinning mockingly. I was not going home. That was quite clear.

The lorry seemed to go right across Berlin. When we finally stopped and I had to get out, we were outside the prison for young women in Berlin-Lichtenberg. Often we had come from Aceta, a cheerful group of friends from work, and gone past to the swimming bath opposite. I recognized the building at once and when the gate shut behind me, I instinctively understood that there was no going back. Alone in my cell, I screamed like a wild animal simultaneously banging my head against the iron on the door.

The interrogations began again. Again and again they wanted to get names from me. I did not name a single name until the day when they fetched me out of the little broom cupboard where they had locked me for three days and nights so that I could 'think things over'; the cupboard was so small and narrow that I could not sit down, and I had just enough air to prevent me from suffocating.

'It's names we want, names! Who was with you in Berlin? Who were you dealing with in Istanbul? Will you be able to remember soon?'

I should say I could remember. In the broom cupboard I had had a good idea, so now they could have as many names as they wanted from me. And I could also give them the appropriate descriptions. All the names which they received from me were the names of people who had died. This was how I betrayed nobody and also protected myself for, since I had after all known the people, I could give accurate descriptions with each name again and again. If I had made up the names and descriptions there would inevitably have been complications or mistakes made during those nocturnal interrogations.

One day, when my despair was even greater than usual, the cell door opened and two men stood before me, one in civilian clothes, the other in uniform. There was food. One of the men tore a page out of a big black book; the other slapped down a handful of stinking fish on to this page and gave it to me. I also received a bowl containing some light brown liquid. It was meant to be coffee. When the door closed again, I stood there still, the paper and the stinking fish in my hand. All I could see were the well-known words of Paul Gerhardt: 'have hope, you poor soul, have hope and be of good courage.' We had often sung this hymn in church; in confirmation classes we had had to learn it by heart where it had never had much meaning for me. But here and now, in my deepest despair, I clung to those words, and they were to sustain me, for ten long years. I cleaned the page as well as I could with the coffee-like liquid; the fish was in any case inedible, and it disappeared at once into the bucket. On the far right-hand side by the window was a square cupboard, upon which a few rays of sunlight fell in the afternoons in spite of the metal plate in front of the window. Up there, I could dry off my Paul Gerhardt hymn. After that the page was carefully folded again and again to disappear into the hem of my dress.

It was August when I was led by a guard into an adjoining cell where a woman lay on the floor. She was bent double, her hands cramped into fists, her fingernails pressed into her palms, her wrists quite white and her lips transparent. I bent over her and asked, 'Can I do anything for you?'

Slowly she opened her large dark eyes. Tears ran down her cheeks. Some time passed before she could speak: 'Please try to open my hands.'

'Does this often happen?' I asked her at the same time trying to open her tightly cramped hands.

'Yes, fairly often. They are tetanus cramps.'

When the attack was over, the guard gave me a sign with his head that I should leave the cell again.

'Something should be done for this woman. She can't possibly be left in a cell on her own,' I begged him.

He snarled at me angrily and led me back to my cell. Left to myself, I tried to pray. What I could not do for myself, I had to do for this woman. That evening there were moves within the prison and I was put into the sick woman's cell and learned she was one of Canaris' last secretaries. Later on I left my wristwatch with her, convinced that she would be allowed to go home sooner than me which was what happened.

'If you get home before I do, please take this watch to my mother. Tell her that I shall definitely come back one day – even if I have to walk all the way from Moscow to Germany.'

Five years later she brought my mother the watch.

In prison, time passed very slowly. One occasional distraction was to sweep the corridor. When it was my turn, I always sang noisily but instead of the words of the song I would sing out my name, my address and a greeting for my mother. I always hoped that another prisoner who might be released before me, would then be able pass on news of me to her. Sometimes, I was taken down four floors to the workshop of a professional tailor, a privileged prisoner, to work as one of the two or three women who helped him each day. He constantly sewed special uniforms or civilian clothing for Russian officers; we women sewed on buttons and made buttonholes. While I was doing this work, I met one of Hitler's secretaries. She looked dreadful, being covered with boils. After some weeks, I did not see her again. It was rumoured that she had gone back to Nuremberg where she was set free shortly after the great trial. The irony of fate!

The former prison for young women was now a general prison holding more men than women. The men would scream beneath the blows of the soldiers whose violence had no use but to add variety to their lives. One morning, when it was again my turn to sweep the corridor, a soldier suddenly opened a cell in front of me and almost pushed me in, while another soldier stood beside me and looked at me with amusement; on the ground in front of me three men were lying naked, completely covered with weals and blood. I started back in horror. I have never heard men laugh so loudly and mockingly as these soldiers did when they closed the cell door.

Many female prisoners were raped. When it was my turn, I said that I had syphilis which put them off. They feared this disease like the plague.

My cell, like all the others, was painted a glossy garish green but everywhere the word 'why' had been scratched in – a word I blocked out of my mind. There was never an answer to it. I wanted to survive, not to go mad. The 100-watt bulb, which burned day and night, was reflected in the garish green wall. Now and again we tried to block out the light, but never succeeded for long; a soldier would come in cursing and screaming to tear down the rags which we had hung over the bulb. The soldiers were often drunk and then they would go brawling from one cell to another, dealing out blows and kicks. I trembled when one evening four of these fellows appeared in my cell, but shouted at the top of my voice: 'Syphilis! Syphilis!' Full of revulsion and disgust and cursing loudly, they departed, and the cell was again shut from the outside. They went into the next cell, where there was a nineteen-year-old girl …

Our main food was a kind of potato soup, or more accurately, potato-peel soup. My cell mate and I thought up a game; we spat patterns of potato peel on to the garish green wall, so that there gradually appeared a pattern in relief, and because of this the garish green colour lost something of its harshness. We laughed about it, in spite of all the terrible things that were going on around us. I was living more consciously and more intensely now that I had nothing more to lose, now that I had nothing left except my life.

Meanwhile September arrived; interrogations ceased and it poured with rain. A soldier brought me my handbag with my lipstick still in it.

'Make yourself as pretty as you can!' he ordered me. He even brought me a shoe brush, pointing with it to my boots which certainly needed cleaning. A prison van was waiting for us in front of the gaol. I was directed to get in, a soldier sat down beside me, and we drove off, crisscrossing through Berlin until we finally arrived at the Soviet headquarters. The soldier led me to a large, ground floor room where I was left on my own until an officer came out of a concealed door that had been camouflaged with wallpaper. Speaking fluent German, he asked me to follow him into the next room where he sat down behind his desk placing me opposite him.

'Do you want to earn a lot of money?' he said in excellent German.

Then came the nub of the matter. I could go to Moscow, where I would be fitted out with decent clothes and amply provided with money, and then travel on to Tokyo. There was only one condition: I was to take a little transmitter with me, so that I should not get out of practice, as it were.

'Do you accept our proposal, Miss Goldacker?'

Without hesitating for even a second, I answered disdainfully: 'I have just got to know Soviet prisons. That's enough for me. I have no wish to see inside Japanese prisons.'

'Does that mean that you are rejecting our proposal?' he asked frostily.

'Yes, that's what it means!'

'On your own head be it, then,' he said, opening the concealed door which led to the next room. He went to the exit, summoned the soldier who had accompanied me and said a few words to him. I was taken back to the Lichtenberg prison.

That same night I was sentenced. The room had been arranged as a courtroom, its walls hung with red cloth, its tables covered with red, the faces of the officers and soldiers red – everything there seemed to be red. Two soldiers sitting to one side were introduced as my witnesses. I had never seen them before, nor presumably had they seen me. The interpreter sat next to them. I went towards the only empty chair in the room and was about to sit down when I heard a shouted, 'You're to remain standing.'

It was about eleven o'clock at night. The trial would last two hours. I had already become so weak with constant hunger that I often used to faint in my cell or outside in the corridor. I stood then in front of this crowd, wretched and hungry, with a chair behind me on which I was not allowed to sit. I had only one wish; that I should not faint here. No, they should not see my weakness. During the trial only Russian was spoken. I did not know my crime as the interpreter only translated now and again, inadequately.

After about an hour I was sent into the small corridor in front of the courtroom until the vast quantities of sandwiches and drinks which had been carried past me had been consumed inside the room by my judges. I could hear the clinking of the glasses, their loud conversation and their peals of laughter. And I was dying of hunger.

When they had finished, they called me in to hear the sentence being pronounced: ten years hard labour. I just shrugged my shoulders. I was allowed to give voice to one last request, like someone condemned to death. I asked if I might inform my mother of my sentence.

'No, ask for something else!' the answer came.

'I have no other request. I just want to tell you that you have as much right to condemn every German man and woman as you have to condemn me here today – that is to say, no right at all!' Without receiving a reply, I was led away to my cell.

I was taken to that wing of the prison where those condemned to death were housed, waiting to be executed or pardoned. I particularly remember a tall, dark-haired woman. She was a Russian by birth and had lived a long time in Vienna. She was waiting for her pardon. One morning I found her bra and knickers in the guardroom; she had been executed.

My cell was not outwardly different from those which had previously imprisoned me: bright green walls, a plank bed on the left, the inevitable bucket, facing the door a window nailed up with metal, to the right a little cube-shaped cupboard, and opposite the bed a small table and a stool. And yet everything was different. In the other cells I had hoped to be set free. Now I knew that there were ten years' hard labour in front of me. I wept and prayed; I did try to pray. As I could find no words of my own, I tried the Lord's Prayer. I never got further than the words, 'Thy will be done.' I wanted my will to be done. It was years before I could say the prayer right through. In that particular cell it was impossible for me.

Once, when I was crying again, the cell door was opened and Boris was standing outside. Boris was a 'criminal' prisoner who helped with the distribution of the food and had just come to give me his big, red and white spotted handkerchief. 'You mustn't cry,' he said in his broken German. 'It's true you've got ten years, but you'll see, you'll be back home again in two or three years.'

How comforting were these well-intentioned words and this human warmth of feeling! I learned later that what he said was absolutely correct as far as 'criminal' prisoners were concerned; it was only for political prisoners that there were no amnesties. I can still see him in front of me: his bright eyes as blue as the sky on a hot summer's day, his hair the colour of ripe wheat, his broad, consoling smile. He came from Lake Baikal in Siberia.

They led us away to the showers. I ought to have been pleased, for I had become completely infested with lice. Yet I was reluctant to go there. In the course of the long walk from the fourth floor down to the bath quarters, which were on the ground floor, I could not help thinking about what my fellow countrymen had done to the Jews. Having arrived downstairs, we had to strip in the little anteroom and we went naked into the shower room. No, I wanted to live. How surprised I was when I actually felt water trickling over my body! It was not gas.

Only male prisoners had the right to a daily walk. When I was in another cell, whose windows had not yet been nailed up with metal, I could see the men. Once a day they used to turn in their sad circles, one behind the other, their arms folded behind their backs. A twelve or thirteen-year-old boy stood in the midst of them like an animal tamer and hit at them with a long whip. He laughed out loud when the men screamed. Was this boy already a prisoner, one of the criminals, perhaps? Or the son of an officer?

On my twenty-sixth birthday, I had spent five weeks in the prison, in solitary confinement, but when I was escorted back to my cell from the morning walk to the WC, I found in my coat pocket a large piece of white bread, cut into slices.

'The day is starting well,' I thought, and was pleased.

When breakfast was being distributed, Boris was standing by the side of the soldier in front of my cell door, and his kind face was beaming. I knew then who had put the slices of bread into my coat pocket. I smiled gratefully. At lunchtime there was again a surprise; instead of the usual tin bowl with the potato-peel soup I was given a proper plate with a big piece of meat and runner beans, and there were even potatoes. For dessert I had a green, unripe apple – the best apple I had ever had. In the afternoon we had a chance to exchange a few words without being observed.

'The bread was from you, wasn't it?'

'Yes, and I cut it because Germans cut their bread into slices and don't break it as we do.'

'Thank you, Boris. And the lunch?'

'That was mine; I wasn't hungry today.'

'That's not true, Boris, but thank you!'

'It is your birthday today, isn't it?'

He had looked through the list of prisoners in the guardroom.

The church bells (there was a church directly adjoining the prison) were just striking ten at night when Boris suddenly called from the corridor, 'Are you asleep, Kurnossaya?'

'No, Boris, what is it?'

'I only wanted to say good night to you, that's all.'

'How nice of you, Boris. Is there any special reason?'

'Yes. I had a pass out so I went to the pub opposite. People there were singing and shouting and laughing, but I couldn't help thinking of you sitting here, sad and lonely in your cell. Then I couldn't stand it any longer with the others and came back.'

'Goodnight, Boris!'

'Good night, Kurnossaya!'

In the autumn of 1945, I was still sitting alone in my cell when one evening my cell door was opened at an unusual time and a man, a soldier, made his way in. The door was shut behind him at once. I heard the sound of the key being turned in the lock. I looked at the man and recognized him as one of my two witnesses.

'So they are beginning all over again,' I thought with horror and at the same moment started to shout out, 'Syphilis!'

'Hush, be quiet! You are wrong, that's not what I'm here for. I want to help you. You'll soon be taken away from here, to where it is very cold. Give me your mother's address. Take this pencil and paper. Write a greeting to her and let me bring you winter clothes. You can't go to Siberia in a summer dress!'

Apart from the grey summer dress I still had my light coat. Should I trust him? Did he only want my mother's address which I had kept secret? Perhaps he really was honest and wanted to help me so I wrote a few words to my mother and gave him the scrap of paper again. He had brought me a few cigarettes, three or four slices of sausage and some bread, all neatly and cleanly wrapped up in newspaper. He then knocked on the cell door, which was opened straightaway, and disappeared without a sound.

That year it was already cold in October. We stood in the prison yard – forty-two women in the midst of hundreds of men. We women were pressed into a comer. The wretched men, wrapped in rags and wasted to skeletons, were herded together like animals. Soldiers were standing about, waiting for orders. Suddenly I saw my witness among them. He was standing on a flight of steps rather higher than the others and seemed to be looking for someone in the group of women. Then he caught sight of me.

He came slowly towards the group of women, moving in a large curve in order not to attract attention. He quickly took two loaves of white bread from under his uniform coat and passed then over to me. Then he said softly and very quickly: 'I've not been able to visit your mother.'

In front of my eyes he tore up the note which I had intended for my mother and had entrusted to him. He disappeared just as quickly and unobtrusively as he had come. I had already hidden the bread – and to think that I was never to know his name.

Lorries covered with large tarpaulins drove into the prison yard, and about twenty prisoners at a time were loaded on to one of them. When the right number was reached, the lorry drove off. The journey was via Karlshorst, Köpenick and Friedrichshagen to Frankfurt an der Oder. It was an endlessly long and sad procession. The air was moist and cold. We went on and on. I sat right at the back of the lorry where the tarpaulin did not reach and shivered in my summer dress. It was a silent procession. Our guards kept their machine guns trained on us, ready to fire. In Frankfurt the men were already standing in front of a big grey building whose walls bore visible traces of the beginnings of decay. My second prison.

One of the women was looking for her son in the men's group. At last she found him, quite close to us. There he was, a tall boy with a child's face, fifteen years old. The Russians had shot his father before his eyes, because he still had a rifle when the Russian troops marched into Berlin. His mother managed secretly to give him half a loaf of white bread that I had given to her for him. We came into our cell: eight wooden beds placed on top of each other for forty-two women. I was shivering and my teeth were chattering. I had an infection and so was allowed more space than my share.

We were given food every other day, a bowl of watery soup and a piece of bread. The confined space and the stench set us all on edge. Some of the women quarrelled continuously, shouting and swearing noisily; one had a larger piece of bread than the other, one was using the bucket while the other was chewing her bread – so it went on.

I was taken three or four times to the doctor, another prisoner;

then the day came on which I was allowed to exercise in the prison yard: ten minutes daily, my hands on my back, just like the men in Berlin-Lichtenberg. Only the small boy lashing out with the whip was missing; instead, soldiers kicked us as we passed by.

When the time came to celebrate the festival of the October Revolution (7 November) the soldiers drank vodka heavily. At dusk, the time we were usually all taken to the WC, a soldier took my hand. Incautiously I had kept Serge's ring on my ring finger.

'Hand it over!' the soldier slurred as he attempted to stand up straight.

Quick as lightning I moved the ring over from one hand to the other, convinced that the soldier, drunk as he was, would not notice.

'What am I supposed to hand over then?' I asked innocently and held my empty hand out before his face.

He slapped me several times in the face. I had to struggle with my tears.

'I suppose you think I am completely drunk. Do you? Hold out your other hand, and be quick!'

He tore the ring away from me.

Next morning I saw in the corner of our cell at the back how a fat Russian woman struggled in vain to force my ring on to her little finger. Her long black hair hung untidily over her blotchy face. She had had sex with the soldier and been given the ring in payment.

It was not a gold ring, but a platinum one. I had an idea, and said: 'You know, that's a completely worthless ring. It's only made of tin. Let me have it back, it means a lot to me.'

'What, it's not worth anything? What a mean trick! Here, have it back!'

I made friends with two young German women. One had been convicted for having been an officer in the army during the war; the other had been arrested because when a soldier had asked her for a bottle of Schnapps (which she did not have) she had given him a bottle of water and had told him that that was better than Schnapps. They were called Maria and Eva, and were taken to Frankfurt every day to do domestic work in the officers' quarters. Later I learnt that once they had had a chance to escape from there – in Frankfurt people spoke German, and would help fellow Germans – but they had stayed because of me. They were afraid of reprisals and feared for me as I was so ill at that time.

The Russian women were better treated than we were, as a matter of course. Their rations of bread or soup were always larger than ours. Some of them also earned extra bread by sleeping with the soldiers. During the daytime, particularly in the evening, they sat on the beds or on the floor of the cell and sang their beautiful, sad songs whose words we did not understand.

When one day we came back to the cell after our ten minutes' walk, one of the Russian women showed me a large old heavy golden crucifix. She had been cleaning the sick people's cell, and an orthodox priest who was on his deathbed had given it to her.

Four weeks after our arrival in Frankfurt we were crowded together in the prison corridor in readiness for the big journey; we were given a complete body search. At that moment death would have been a welcome friend to me.

Although the soldiers searched me, they did not find my Paul Gerhardt poem nor the two gold coins. I had sewn these treasures into the gusset of my knickers, and was holding the ring in my mouth again. When we stepped through the prison gates out into the street, the men were already waiting for us, standing in a long, grey column in the mist, in fives, flanked right and left by soldiers with their machine guns ready to fire. The men's shaven heads looked like skulls.

Maria and Eva supported me. The grey column started moving slowly, then stopped opposite the old hospital. Our faces were as grey as the walls of the weather-worn building. In front of it was a handcart with a rough wooden coffin on it. A man came out of the building and threw the corpse he was carrying into the light-coloured, open coffin.

That was the last thing I saw in Germany.

4

The long, grey procession moved slowly towards the goods station passing bomb craters and ruins. A red goods train waited for us. I counted twenty-seven vans. We women were ordered to halt by one of the last vans of this long train. The sliding door of the van was pushed open and we helped each other to climb in. To the right and left of the sliding door the entire width of the van was taken up with a bed-shaped shelf halfway up, so that standing upright was possible only in the middle of the van, near to the sliding door. The Russian women took the places up on the shelving which meant they could look through the small window in the van, and talk occasionally at stations with free people. The Germans had to lie huddled together beneath the shelving, packed tightly on the floor of the van. In the free space in the middle, where it was possible to stand upright, there was an iron stove which was used just once during our journey. Behind the stove a rectangular hole had been sawn in the floor of the van, as a latrine. There were forty-two women when we set off. A Russian woman was appointed as spokeswoman for the van. She had killed a man, probably her lover. For a long time I thought that she was in her forties, but it turned out she was just twenty years old.

It was impossible to stand around all the time in the middle of the van. The most comfortable position seemed to be to lie bent double beneath the shelving. I was selected by my compatriots to receive and distribute our food and drink.

After we had been checked, counted and searched the whole day long, and as night was falling, the train, at last, started to move slowly. I was relieved. It was better to be travelling, no matter where we went, than to endure the never-ending waiting. In spite of the tragic finality of this moment, which I felt acutely, I was filled with inexplicable curiosity.

The train stopped once daily, often on the open track. A soldier opened the door and brought our food: one slice of dry bread or sometimes only a half slice, a teaspoonful of sugar every few days, and a fish head for us Germans. The fish itself was given to the Russian women, which I could well understand in spite of my hunger. After all, it was their countrymen who were distributing the food.

Occasionally there was water, half a can among nine people. Three and a half gulps for each of us. Thirst tormented us more than hunger, especially as the fish heads were always very salty. Once two girls, both half dead and almost naked, found the energy to have a fight on account of a mouthful of water. The next morning they were both taken into the mortuary van. I always retained a little gulp of water in my mouth, and then spat out the water into my hand, in order to wash myself in a rough and ready way. We were infested with lice.

By the beginning of December, after travelling over a month, for days on end we would not get any water. Because of the cold outside, the walls of the van became coated with frost from our breath; I scratched this frost off with a spoon in order to quench my thirst. Now and again we took snow which had been lying between or near the railway lines and which tasted of oil and coal, but we consumed it avidly. If only we had had a fire in the stove! My light, grey silk dress and my thin summer coat scarcely offered any protection against the icy cold. Fortunately it had been raining on the day of my arrest and I had put on my boots. But the greatest piece of luck was that Maria and Eva had a blanket and two pillows; we placed the pillows on the wooden floor of the van and rolled ourselves together, with the blanket over us like a tent. In this way we kept ourselves warm with our own breath.

Men and women died of starvation and cold or of typhus. We three in our tent promised each other that should one of us catch typhus, she would leave the tent, in order not to give the disease to the other two. It was this tent that saved all three of our lives; both because we could keep each other warm and because it isolated us from the other prisoners.

It was night time and as still as the grave. The train had stopped for days at Brest-Litovsk on the Polish-Russian frontier. Suddenly I heard Eva weeping at my side.

'Why are you crying?'

'I'm so hungry!'

As if we were not all hungry! I was furious, but then I had an idea. A sack full of dry bread hung over us swinging from a nail in the corner of the van. It belonged to the senior person in the van who had shown wise foresight. Well aware of the infinite-seeming extent of her Russian homeland, she had lain in a supply of bread while in prison. Everybody slept. Tossia, the 'senior' Russian woman, was snoring loudly, but one slight sound might wake her. Slowly and cautiously I crept nearer to the sack and almost without making a sound, I took out one piece of bread after another. That whole night long we sucked and chewed at the bread, successfully emptying almost the whole sack without waking anyone. What's more, the bread was as hard as stone.

The next morning we were woken up by loud cursing and swearing. Tossia had discovered the theft and abused us loudly and crudely. I crept out of our 'tent' and placed myself in the centre of the van. I was responsible for the Germans, at least as far as food was concerned, and I had made up my mind to defend them – and thereby also myself. After all, it was a matter of survival. I spoke not without a certain theatrical effect, quietly and firmly, saying: 'We willingly recognize that we are the losers in this war, but that does not mean that we have lost our dignity as well as the war. None of us steals. We are much too proud to misappropriate the belongings of those who have conquered us. Why don't you ask the Russians? Most of them must have known where you stored your bread!'

The best of it was that at the moment of delivering this speech I almost convinced myself that I spoke the truth. Everybody was quiet, even Tossia's abuse was silenced. They believed me. When I crept back again under our blanket and was squatting wedged between Maria and Eva, the latter asked me: 'Where did you get the bread we had last night, then?'

'Hm. From her, of course!'

Even my friends had been convinced by my lie.

Before her arrest Hildegard had lived in Potsdam where she had given music lessons. At sixty-two, she was the oldest of us; transparently thin, she would stand in the middle of the van, dressed only in her petticoat which was black with lice. She held her brown-and-red-checked woollen dress in her hand trying in vain to delouse it. She was the first to die. Eva and I had to bury her hurriedly in the snow, not far from the railway line. When she died she was wearing her long brown winter coat with a fox-fur collar. Why did we bury her in her coat? Surely she didn't need it any more?

Later on the dead were collected up. A big van, much larger than the other vans, had been coupled on to the end of the train. The dead were piled up in it. I seemed to be stronger than the others and had to drag a number of corpses to this van. A short while before the end of our journey it was so full that we had to bend the dead bodies in order to make them fit in.

Our train was held up at the Polish-Russian frontier for two weeks. One night I compared the width of my shoulders with that of our 'hole'. With some effort and self-control I was sure I could force myself through. Eva and Maria were no broader than I was, and we decided to escape together. I did not want to go without them, for they had held back from escaping at Frankfurt for my sake. It was drizzling. Every night the barking of machine guns could be heard, and in the mornings, when the soldiers brought us bread and fish, they told us that a few men had tried to escape the previous night.

'They won't go far. Idiots!' one of the soldiers said.

All the same, I wanted to attempt it. It would have meant an ending, one way or another. One night we seemed to be ready. I crept on all fours to the hole. Maria had followed me.

'Don't go,' she begged, 'they did so much shooting last night.'

I stayed, and later I regretted it. The next morning the train was still waiting at the same spot.

When the train was not moving – and it stopped for seventeen days and nights – the lice tormented us even more fiercely than when we were travelling. On the seventeenth day we were loaded into another train where the broad-gauge railway track began. As we changed trains some prisoners tried to use the twilight to obscure their escape. It was easy for the soldiers to stop them. Through the darkness we heard orders and shouting, the barking of dogs, shooting. Then silence over the snow.

Officers waited for us in the nearby van. It was almost pitch black – two candles flickered making ghost-like shadows dance on the walls of the coach. It was eerie. One of the officers asked for our names. Then we were counted again, one by one. The corpses were also counted. One by one. Whether they were living or dead, the numbers would have to tally finally when we reached our destination. A soldier came and ordered us to get undressed. Then he led us, naked as we were, through the snow to a carriage that was standing apart and which had facilities for washing and disinfecting. We were provided with warm water, and while we were washing ourselves our clothes were disinfected. Each of us was allowed only one bowl of water, and yet it was an almost comfortable feeling to be able to wash at last, after so many weeks. Our disinfected clothes were returned and we were led back into our dark, dirty van. The cold, then the warm water, and again the walk in the cold air made us sleepy. Suddenly the van door opened, and a heavy object was shoved into the middle of the van. The door was closed. Silence. And in the silence, an uncanny, disjointed knocking. Maria asked: 'Where's Erika? Have you seen her?'

'No, I haven't seen her here. She was still around while we were washing.'

I crept in the direction of the ghostly knocking and bumped into something cold and soft. It was Erika beating with her cold, bare feet in a regular rhythm against the van door. She had stayed behind in the coach where we had washed, without our noticing. Naked and already half-dead, she had then tried to find our van, until she had collapsed in the snow exhausted. Then a soldier had pushed her into the van. Before dying in my arms, she regained consciousness and called out my name in a strange, changed voice.

That was on 16 December, my brother's birthday.

The next morning a soldier asked how many dead we had in the van. 'One,' I replied.

'We'll come back again tomorrow, when there are more.'

They took our dying for granted. It was quite unremarkable.

He was right: two days later there were three dead bodies to be removed; that made it worthwhile. On the way to the mortuary van we were accompanied by a soldier who cracked his long whip incessantly; we were going too slowly for him, though we could scarcely drag ourselves along at all. The train moved on.

Sometimes the train stopped at a station. Then people came along from all directions, hoping that we might be able to tell them something about their own missing or deported relatives. Others came in order to do some unscrupulous bartering with the starving prisoners. The girl who had obtained the heavy gold crucifix in prison in Frankfurt bartered it for a loaf of bread. I exchanged my two gold coins for three kilograms of bread, but it was white bread!

I shared out the bread with the people down below who lay with me on the floor of the van.

We travelled further north. We became ever weaker and more wretched with hunger and cold. Every day one of us died. The Russian women were much stronger than we were and could hold out longer. They also had more to eat. I kept on moving my toes a hundred times on end, so that they would not freeze. I had read about that somewhere in a prison story. When a Russian woman stole my boots, I was too weak to prevent her from taking them.

Lena, a German and a lesbian, had made obvious sexual approaches to me from the start, when we were in prison in Frankfurt. She entertained us with playing cards which she had made, I have no idea how. She told our fortunes using the cards and maintained that I should eventually come back home, after a long time, and that three old ladies would be waiting for me. Who were the three ladies supposed to be, then? She herself would come to grief. 'You will leave me here,' she used to say.

She was eventually stricken with typhus and spent all her time squatting over the hole. She had a high fever. As she lay dying she called me to her, but Maria held me back. 'Don't go too close to her, she will try to embrace you and tomorrow you will have typhus!'

'Come to me,' Lena panted with her dying voice that already seemed half to come from another world.

And then: 'Come close to me. Help me! My arm is getting longer and longer.'

And again Maria held me back: 'She wants to kiss you. You'll see, you'll have caught it by tomorrow.'

And then, I do not know why, I answered the dying woman, whose feet I touched with my feet, in a voice that was as cold as that of the soldier who had inquired about the number of the dead and who said he would come back for them the next day, when it would be worth his while. 'The longer your arm, the easier for you to scratch your lousy back with it!'

She understood, and cursed me before she died.

An hour later another woman died. Her last words were directed to her hairdresser: 'How annoying, I made an appointment at the hairdresser's and could not cancel it. And it is so difficult to find a hairdresser nowadays but I really couldn't help it.'

And that was all.

On 4 January the train finally came to a halt. Where were we? In Siberia? The van door was pushed open. We, the survivors, looked grey and yellow. We were filthy and lousy. For two months we had been faring worse than animals. I had retrieved a pair of shoes from a fellow prisoner. She could not put them on any more as her feet had been completely frozen.

We came out into the icy cold. I wore only my light, grey dress and my thin summer coat. We were loaded, one by one, onto the waiting lorries. We huddled as closely together as possible underneath the tarpaulin. When the lorries eventually stopped, we found ourselves in front of the great gatehouse of a camp of huts. We were directed into one of these wooden huts, the bath house. We had to hand over our clothes to be disinfected in an anteroom. In the bathroom we were each given a wooden tub which was filled and then re-filled with water. After I had washed myself with the red soft soap I voluptuously let the water run over my emaciated body; with the second tub of water I washed my hair. Innumerable little black dots were floating on the soapy water: lice, as usual!

We were all terrifyingly thin. I looked down at myself and thought that I was looking at the body of a ten-year-old girl – no breasts, no pubic hair, no menstruation any more. My body looked like that of a starving little girl.

Back in the anteroom we were brought coarse linen pyjamas. A hairdresser, a prisoner like ourselves, shaved our heads. The last vestige of femininity was taken from us. When it was my turn, a few tears ran down my cheeks. The hairdresser noticed, shaved the back of my head and left me a little tuft of hair in the front.

'Put a scarf over your head, so that the others won't notice straight away that you still have a little hair!' was all he said. Then we were taken to a hut with a corridor in the middle and two-tiered bedsteads on either side. Three of us had to lie down in a place which would have just been sufficient for two. Eva, Maria and I naturally stayed together. Separated from me by a narrow passageway a girl was lying by herself on a bed; it was she who had given me her shoes and whose frozen legs were already beginning to putrefy. Her shins were black and oozed pus. It was possible to see through to the bones. The three of us changed our positions every day so that each of us should have a turn on the warm spot in the middle. The inner side of the door into our hut was covered with frost; we felt the cold deep down within ourselves.

The first evening they brought us fish soup. I have never eaten such wonderful fish soup, and I wanted to make a note of the recipe at once. For two months on end we had been living on dry bread and a few fish bones, and this was our first warm soup! The containers holding the soup which was brought to us had been made out of empty tin cans. The name of the firm could still be made out: 'Oscar Meyer, Chicago. Tinned meat'. 'I must make sure I write to this man Oscar Meyer when I get back. He ought to know what use can still be made in Russia of his "wrapping paper"!' I said to my friends. How often I have thought even years later of that wonderful fish soup; no soup has tasted so good to me since then!

Inside the huts where we lived there were, of course, no toilets. We often had to walk half a kilometre or more to get to them. In this camp the latrine – a piece of wood with six holes – was fortunately only about 100 metres' distance from our hut.

I went out. In spite of the white snow it was a pitch-black night. An icy wind was blowing. I could scarcely stand up against it. I fought my way forwards, walking half-asleep. Deathly stillness, only the whistling of the wind. The lavatory door was open, and I had scarcely shut it after me when one large hand covered my mouth while another clasped my arm and pushed me against the frozen lavatory wall. The man was stronger than I was. I could not scream. He pressed me even harder against the wall, let go my arm and tried to put his paw between my legs. With an almost superhuman burst of strength I succeeded in tearing myself away from the fellow in spite of my weakness. When I was back in my bed I started to tremble and weep. The senior person in the hut wanted to know what was wrong. I never said anything about it and never found out who it was.

Very soon I no longer had the strength to hold my spoon. I no longer wished to eat. Oh, to die and as quickly as possible! At that, Maria took my spoon and fed me like a child. I was ashamed of my weakness; it was no easier for her than it was for me. How could I let myself give up like that? Life goes on, it must.

For three weeks, we only left our beds to go to the lavatory, and I never went there on my own again. Then we were taken (as always, at night, and in covered lorries) to another camp, Sangorodok, the hospital camp for all the camps around Inta.

As on our arrival at the first camp, we were taken to the bath premises immediately. We had to get undressed in a room with wooden benches along the walls to the right and left. All I had were the linen pyjamas given to me at the other camp; my light, grey summer dress had not survived the disinfection process but had disintegrated into a thousand rags. As for my summer coat, it had changed owner.

The bathroom resembled that of the first camp: big taps for hot and cold water in the middle. A tall man in charge standing nearby distributed water – two tubs each. Anyone with very long hair was allowed three tubfuls. My little tuft of hair did not entitle me to a third tub.

Two nurses, who were also prisoners, busied themselves with the girl with the frostbitten legs. They washed her and then carried her into the hut for severely ill patients. When we finally arrived at this hut, it had already been prepared for the operation, and the Lithuanian doctor, also a prisoner, amputated both her legs below the knees.

Maria and I were put into the room next to hers, which almost dazzled us when slowly we entered it. After months in the van we had forgotten that a room could be so bright, friendly and clean. In the room, there were eight beds with white sheets and brightly-coloured bedspreads, four on each side. There were even pillows there with pillowslips. Maria lay in the bed next to mine, and between the beds were bedside tables. And there, standing on the bedside table facing me was a bunch of flowers! Really? Flowers? No, that was impossible; they were only bare twigs decorated with bright bits of wool.

The other girls looked at us newcomers curiously. They talked to us, they talked amongst themselves; they talked and talked. We lay there, looked at them and kept silent; we did not understand a word. I was freezing alone in my bed. Maria was also shivering with cold so I crept into her bed and snuggled up closely to her as if I were in the van, and we cried because it was so lovely here in this room.

Later we got to know all our roommates: Ira, Dunia, Shura, Nadia, Tania and Katia with the tattooed breasts who belonged to an organized gang of robbers. Previously they had all been in the camps around Sangorodok. Shura had broken her leg. She had fallen down from one of the many watchtowers. As a criminal prisoner she was allowed to take the place of a soldier in a watchtower. Ira, the teacher from Leningrad, was already a grandmother at thirty-six (the three generations were in prison); she was very beautiful and full of vitality in spite of her tuberculosis. She told us wonderful stories and related novels to us which she had read in 'the life that had gone before'. Maria and I watched her mouth and her expressive face as she recounted the stories with her mellifluous voice in the evenings. How beautiful was her big, broad face! Some words and phrases were repeated; we remembered them and tried to make use of them ourselves. How pleased I was when I could completely understand one of her stories for the first time. I only understood them when I was looking at her. For a long time I needed to have her facial expression in order to understand what she was saying. Very gradually and cautiously we too began to talk, and they all listened to us attentively, with wide open eyes. They showed great pity when they learnt where we came from.

'Do your relatives know where you are?'

'No, nobody knows where we are.'

'Have you been able to write home yet?'

'How are we to write? We have no paper, no pencil, no stamps.'

'You are even poorer than we are.'

When I had recovered somewhat, I was allowed to work as an orderly in this hospital hut. I could still sleep in the small bed on top of the sack of wooden shavings. I had a coverlet and a pillow. What bliss! The rough wooden floor of the patients' rooms as well as the wide corridor between them had to be scrubbed bright and shining every day. I used all my energy, working quickly, thoroughly and well. I did not want to lose my bed.

One morning when I was scrubbing the floor of one of the men's rooms – there were twelve patients in that room – one of the men tried to feel my breast as I was about to wipe under his bed.

'Don't touch me!' I shouted.

'Don't tell me you are still a virgin!'

'Let me be, you swine!'

He did not let me be, and I slapped his face with my floorcloth; I had not had time to wring out the cloth, and as it slapped, dirty water was sprayed around.

'You miserable whore! I'll teach you how to behave in the camp.'

'Shut up, you idiot, and let me get on with my work.'

He threw himself upon me. As we both rolled around on the floor, the other patients creased over with laughter.

Even after I had freed myself and was racing along to the women's room, I still heard him shouting behind me, 'I'll kill you, you German whore!'

'If Sasha says that he will kill you, he will have to do it, or else he'll be killed by one of his gang. You can't stay here. Hide in the attic.'

It was Nadia who gave me this advice, and I straightaway hid in the attic. At nightfall – it was one of those bright, clear, greenish nights which precede the white nights – I ventured out of my hiding place and crept into my bed. In spite of my anxiety, I had just managed to get to sleep when somebody shook me roughly by the shoulder: 'Get up. Pack your things together. You're leaving Sangorodok now.'

The day before, I had received a black working dress which I put on the over my pyjamas. The canvas shoes with leather toecaps and heels went on my bare feet, and instead of a coat I put on a wadded jacket that was dirty and full of holes. Who knows how many prisoners had already worn this jacket before me? It was stiff with dirt! The soldier and I left Sangorodok – and my friends – like thieves in the night.

No other camp was willing to take me.

'We don't want any political prisoners here.'

'You are bringing a fifty-eighter? No, there's no room here for politicals.'

That night I must have heard these and similar sentences at least ten times. My 'escort' became more and more angry as we went from camp to camp, while I became ever more light-hearted and cheerful; if nobody wanted me, I had to go back to where I came from. Early in the morning, before reveille, we were outside Sangorodok again. The admission formalities were quickly dealt with; after all, I had already been accepted here in spite of my 'Paragraph 58'. When I came back into the women's room, everybody embraced me: Nadia, Shura, Ira and all the others. How happy I was to see them again!

To prevent the worst happening, it was easier to send Sasha, the bandit, away from Sangorodok that very day; he, a bandit, was acceptable everywhere. I learnt later that Nadia was right; the members of the gang which he led did kill him – with a big kitchen knife.

Near to Sangorodok, about 800 metres away, a new camp was being built. We could see from a distance that the new huts were bigger than those we lived in.

'What sort of people is this camp intended for?' I asked.

'For prisoners like us here, those who are no longer ill enough to be in bed and at the same time not well enough to be sent to the coalmines. A kind of convalescent camp,' Ira informed me.

Ira, the others and I were taken to the new camp before it was even finished. The huts were cold and very damp. We consisted of only 17 women, accommodated in a small section of a hut; in the large huts there were about 2,000 men – that is, if these wretched figures could still be described as men.

It was here that I met an Austrian baron who then seemed more dead than alive. He was very tall, skeletal and completely demoralized. He knew the Gestapo headquarters at the Schwedenplatz in Vienna as he had been imprisoned there after the attempted assassination of Hitler. He was as much in despair as I had been at the start of my imprisonment in Berlin-Lichtenberg. I told him about my Paul Gerhardt poem. He did not know it. So I removed it from the hem of my dress and gave it to him; he had greater need of it now than I had. He was shivering with cold. I would have to think of something to help him. I soon had an opportunity; one Sunday morning I was sent together with other girls to the washhouse to patch up pyjamas. Sonia, who was responsible for the washhouse, took no notice of us after she had thrown the torn pyjamas to us. It was no wonder; her camp husband, a criminal prisoner, had come from another camp to pay her a visit. Criminal prisoners were given these sorts of privileges. For instance, they could work as lorry drivers which meant they could get into other camps with a special pass. While the couple were occupied with their own affairs in a small adjoining room, I picked out the best pair of underpants which I could find in a hurry. They were a long, stout pair of underpants, roughened on the inside. Quick as a flash, I made them disappear into the sleeve of my jacket.

'I shall be back right away. If Sonia asks about me, I've just gone outside.'

'Hurry up. She'll be back any time now!'

I had the baron summoned from his hut. He came at once. I looked round. Nobody saw us.

'Quick, hide these underpants and don't let anybody see them or take them off you, else we're both in trouble!'

He hurriedly took them, thanked me and survived.

Every day several men died in this so-called convalescent camp. I was taken ill with typhus. Each time I was delirious I had the same dream; I saw Lena, the lesbian woman who had cursed me before she died in the van of the train. I saw her unnaturally large dark-brown eyes in her bright face that was encircled by snow-white hair. She threw the thermometer at me like an arrow. I had a temperature of over 40°C. Nadia and Eva nursed me. They went out with me to the lavatory where the dead Lena was always lying in wait for me with her thermometer-spear. At last the day came when Lena and her thermometer were no longer there. My temperature went down. I began to live again.

Weak as I was, thin as a skeleton and more starved than ever, I had the unusual luck of being allocated to kitchen work. I was placed in the scullery which lay between the main kitchen and the dining room. Hundreds of dirty aluminium dishes were pushed at me from the dining room through a small window; I had to wash them quickly and very superficially, since Grisha, the cook, was waiting to fill them for the waiting prisoners. If I wanted to keep this job, where I had enough to eat, I would have to work quickly and for long hours. At that time I fainted at least once a day from hunger and malnutrition, but up to then I had been lucky; no one in the big kitchen had noticed anything. I was very frightened that I should be dismissed from kitchen work, when all that I was suffering from was lack of food. One day when I came round again after fainting, I saw through a red veil a group of people around me. I must have fallen on to one of the giant cooking pots. There were splashes of blood everywhere, and blood flowed from my broken nose for a long time. In the hospital hut the Lithuanian doctor stitched up my wounded nose without an anaesthetic. Naturally, I lost my good job.

5

The Russian prisoners seemed able to endure camp life more easily than we foreigners. For hundreds of years, prison, banishment and forced labour have been a part of the life of the Russian people. Every Russian family had or had had a relative in prison. There was a saying circulating, which would cost anyone overheard speaking it ten years' hard labour: 'Russian people are divided into three categories: those who are in prison, those who have been in prison and those who will be in prison.'

Because, there were so many more male than female prisoners, every woman had a 'companion' who protected her from the other men. Without one, she was fair game for all of the men. I lived with a Cossack, Ivan Ivanovich Shestakov. For a long time he let me think that he was as much a political prisoner as I was. But he was so skilful at theft and deception that I very soon doubted his political 'paragraph'.

For a time we worked together in the hospital hut until he was put in charge of the bath hut and washhouse. Soon afterwards he had me transferred to join him there. One day he rushed in laughing, looked quickly round to check we were alone, and then took from his trouser pocket a dress which seemed to get longer and longer.

'Unpick it quickly and alter it,' he said laughing. This was unnecessary advice; I knew it had to become unrecognizable. On another occasion he came to me panting as he dragged along a whole pillowcase full of meat. I thought that he had brought red soft soap. That was what Ivan Ivanovich was like; he would do anything for me. Our guards generally overlooked relationships between men and women in the camp, provided they were more or less stable ones. Many of the camp men came into the women's huts overnight. Even this was tacitly tolerated. I did not like this and preferred to go to Vanya in the bath hut. How often we fought! He was furiously jealous, but he protected me from the other men.

In the middle of the ironing room in the bath hut there was a large linen cupboard. On its left, was the door to the washhouse, opposite was the large oven for the irons, and next to it against the wall and beneath the window was a long narrow table for ironing, folding up and collecting together laundry. Between the back of the linen cupboard and the wall of the hut, separated from the rest of the room by a curtain, were a wooden bed, a tiny table and two stools; here Ivan Ivanovich slept. And so very often, did I. We stayed together for three years.

How fortunate I was to be working inside the camp and not to be outside in the cold all day! It was November when the thermometer registered between 35 and 40 degrees below freezing point. Ivan Ivanovich would occasionally come into the hospital hut to fetch patients to be bathed. Or else he just came to see me. One evening he came just before roll call. I saw immediately that he was seething with rage. He hit me as if he had lost his reason. I was wearing the dress he had stolen for me. It was a blue check, with a long, brightly coloured sash. I had worked on it with such pleasure; any bright piece of thread I came across I pulled out – for my sash. I wanted it to be bright and cheerful. That evening Ivan had learnt that I had sent greetings to a former patient from Sangorodok whom I had nursed for a time, through another patient who had been sent into the same camp. This was enough to infuriate Ivan with jealousy and rage. He hit me harder and harder until I had no strength left to resist. At the same time I would have killed him gladly if only I had been able to. How I loathed this life! It was enough to make you sick. And still, there were eight more years of this life to endure. No. I did not want any more.

I washed the blood off my face, let myself be counted with the others, and then went out into the cold and the snow. At the other end of the hut there was a ladder that led up to the loft. I knew the loft well. A person could be alone there, and I had already been up there a few times when I had been tired of the chatter around me. That was how I came to know about the big nail. I found it quite easily in the dark. My lovely sash! I folded it in two, for it had to hold firm. Nobody had seen me go up. Nobody would notice my absence before the next roll call, early in the morning. Ivan would surely think that I had gone howling to the women's hut; no one would notice my absence there either. Here was the big nail. If only it were not so cold. I shivered in my cotton dress. I didn't care. Of course, the sash would hold. And the nail. I was determined to make an end to this miserable life. And yet there was this fear, fear of finality, fear of the cold, fear of dying, fear of the frozen earth in which I would be buried, with a piece of birch wood attached to my big toe; on the birch wood would be my name and '58/6', the number of the paragraph of this strange law according to which I had been sentenced. If only I didn't have this fear. It was greater than my despair, and stronger than any feeling of loathing. Fear and cold boring into my breasts and my body compelled me to go down below, into the warmth of the women's hut.

The next morning I went as usual to work in the hospital hut; Ivan Ivanovich came as usual, fetched patients to be bathed, and greeted me with a laugh as if nothing had happened.

I became ill. I shook with the cold. A high temperature again. A skull in every corner of the room. They stared at me and pursued me in my fevered dreams. My high temperature refused to come down. I was ill for a very long time and taken to another hut. Every day Ivan brought me milk and small pieces of butter which he had pilfered somewhere or other. Finally, the skulls, which hung staring at me from the corners of the room, slowly faded, and in their place I saw a gleaming, golden bow which led to the sky like a bridge.

He saved my life, as he had done once before when I had been just as ill. However, I never let myself be struck again without hitting back, and this surprised him very much.

'A Russian woman would not dare to raise her hand against the man who strikes her,' he said.

Ivan continued to visit me almost every day. 'You know,' he said, 'I am a man, and a man needs a woman. I was looking for one while you were still ill. I don't want you to hear about it from other people, and so I am telling you myself. But I want to tell you too that you are my lawful wife and that you are the one I want.'

What did I care?

A few days later Marlene, who worked as a nursing orderly in the hut where I now was, woke me up holding a cigarette in front of my nose. She had rolled it herself, of course: a piece of newspaper, from Pravda preferably, filled with machorka.

'Why don't you try smoking again? Perhaps you'll like it!'

Marlene was right; I just had to try it again. I took the roll-up and

I liked it! To make sure I did not disturb the other patients, I blew the smoke underneath the bed clothes; but where was the ash to go? Then I caught sight of a small Oskar Meyer tin at the bedside of my neighbour, a middle-aged woman. This was just what I was looking for but I had scarcely flicked the ash into it before my neighbour attacked me angrily: 'What do you think you're doing, you slut? Have you ever seen such cheek? No sooner has she blown in than she thinks that she can do what she likes here!'

'What are you getting so worked up for? Does it matter all that much if I use your ashtray?'

'What's that you say? Ashtray? Did you hear that? She calls this an ashtray. That tin's holding a whole night's worth of spit. I've been really careful collecting enough of that muck to get it taken and analysed in the laboratory. And you silly idiot, you dare to stub your cigarette end in it! Now I'm going to have to start all over again with this spitting business.'

'Oh, I'm sorry! But I really couldn't know that the muck in your tin was meant for the laboratory. You should label your tin next time, so that nobody will be tempted to mistake an Oskar Meyer laboratory container for an Oskar Meyer ashtray.'

She looked at me in amazement, and we both laughed.

'My name is Valentina Semionovna, Valia to my friends. What are you called?'

'Emma Pavlovna. My friends call me Emochka.'

'Where are you from? You have a funny accent.'

At that time I already spoke Russian well enough to be able to hold my own in the language, but I have never lost my German accent. I told her the name of the city I came from.

'Are you a Jew or a German?'

'Why?'

'Because you speak Russian as the Jews do here.'

'Nobody has told me that before!'

'How long is your sentence?'

'Ten years. And yours?'

'I've got ten years too, but I've done seven of them. When did you start your sentence?'

'1945.'

At that time I had just done two years; there were still eight years ahead of me. She only had another three years. In the event, though, it was to be four. One year more or less in prison – what does it matter to the authorities?

'You've still got a great deal to learn, if you want to survive!'

'I know. But first I want to learn Russian so that I'm not recognised as a foreigner right away. And I want to learn to read and write. Now how can anyone do that in here?'

We were forbidden to possess pencil or paper. The authorities were afraid that a word scribbled on a scrap of paper might be the start of a conspiracy against them! Also there were so many illiterates among the prison guards that it was embarrassing for them to find something that they could not read. On one later occasion a woman prison guard found me with a poem which I had copied from a volume of Lermontov. She held the sheet of paper in her hand just as I used to hold my mother's newspaper when I was four years old – upside down.

'Will you allow me?'

I approached her, took the piece of paper out of her hand, turned it round and gave it back to her. Red with anger, she rushed out of the hut, followed by our mocking laughter.

But at that time, I was the one who had to study. Valia was angelically patient with me. She had no German, it is true, but had learnt the Roman alphabet and so could teach me the Cyrillic script. Every day she taught me for a few hours. Between the two of us we had a tiny pencil and a few pages of writing paper torn out of a pad when its owner had gone outside.

In the summer of 1954, during the tenth year of my sentence, the government decided to set up schools in the labour camps and to provide Russian language courses, for both Russians and foreigners. 'Better late than never,' I said to myself and was happy to be sitting in a school desk again, to be given paper and pencil, and to be learning once more. But at that time, I had to work in secret with Valia – Valia, my friend, who was so ill and yet could still recite long poems during the evenings or recount novels. She knew the whole of Pushkin's

Emmy with her mother

Emmy with her mother in 1955

Emmy's father Dr Paul Goldacker

Emmy in 1941

Emmy with her husband

Inta prison camp 1950

Eugene Onegin by heart; it was from her too that I learned my first Lermontov poems.

In each of the many camps where I stayed during my ten-year sentence there was a library: a quiet, pleasant and often very small room where smoking and talking were forbidden. You could find there translations from English, especially Dickens; there were also Russian editions of French writers such as Mérimée, Maupassant, Anatole France or Victor Hugo. It was not often you came across translations from German. I only found two volumes, one work by Heinrich Heine and one by Schiller.

However, cultural life in the camp was not restricted to books. Once a month we were shown a film in the dining room. These were usually Russian films, of course; but we also saw Hungarian, Czech or Polish films. The best of all the films I saw there was The *Count of Monte Cristo* in the original French version. I saw this film five times, which was not all that easy; the dining room was much too small to hold us all at once, so we went hut by hut. For five evenings I 'lived' every evening in a different hut. I was lucky that none of the prison guards noticed what I was up to!

Every camp had a so-called 'culture brigade' which mostly consisted of professional actresses, singers or dancers. For a long time, we were fortunate enough to enjoy the dancing skills, the charm and the grace of Tamara V, a former prima ballerina at the Kiev opera house. She trained many young prisoners as dancers during her time in prison. Thanks to the artistes who were with us in the camp, it was possible to perform whole operas, such as Bizet's *Carmen* or Gounod's *Faust*. We who formed the audience – and I believe there never was a more grateful audience – were enthusiastic. These musicians did not have scores, but wrote out the notes from memory. The instruments consisted of only a violin, a few guitars, a concertina, and sometimes a mouth organ. But for us, these concert or opera evenings were fabulously lovely. Suddenly we were in another world, and, for a short time, prison existence fell away from us. The most skilled of us helped to make costumes and scenery, which were put together, with more imagination than materials, from coloured paper, dyed cloth, old chairs or tables.

Easter! Easter in the Russian style! Valentina Semionovna invited me to her hut. How could she do this? She never received parcels, she could not work, and yet she was inviting me to a celebration! She was even poorer than we Germans. Nobody wrote to her, nobody at all. And yet at that Easter festivity she had something which she shared with me. On the small table beside her bed was a gleaming and cheerfully embroidered small cloth of a type that is often seen in Russia. On it were two huge onions, a piece of bread – at least a pound – and a succulent herring glistening in an Oskar Meyer dish. Wherever had she acquired all this? I never found out. She shared this Easter meal with me and did so with the gracious, formal, generous and yet delicate gestures which are typical of the hospitality of her people. What she offered was insignificant, but the way she offered it, I shall never forget. She invited me to a festive meal and treated me like a queen.

I did not cease to learn from Valia. One day, after she had spent many weeks in bed, she was allowed to get up again. She stood in the middle of the ward, tall and thin. She had not washed herself, and her long, wispy grey hair hung untidily about her pale face which bore signs of ageing. We all thought she was tubercular. She seemed to be much more ill than everybody else. That day a team of inspectors was expected from Moscow. I was already feeling very much better, and, as soon as I had got up, I went out to wash myself.

'Can anyone lend me a comb?' I asked when I came back. And then: 'Aren't you going to have a wash as well, Valia?'

'Let me tell you something, Emochka. If you wash yourself and do your hair, you will feel good and you will also look well. That will only give your dear fellow prisoners cause for jealousy. Then the doctors and the inspectors will come, and they will find that a political prisoner looking as good as you cannot be left in hospital any longer and so, very soon, you will be going back to general work outside. But if you look like me – pale, dirty and uncared-for – nobody will take any notice of you. Everybody – doctors, inspectors and prisoners – will be happy to see you weak and wretched. If you look as bad as this, you might perhaps be lucky and stay even longer in the hospital hut.'

How right she was, how very, very right!

'I shall tell you something else,' she continued: 'The day will come when you can't work any more; you will be exhausted and weary, but no doctor will give you a medical certificate for that, yet you do need a few days' rest if you are to survive. That's when you need to help yourself.'

And then she showed me how I could help myself.

'You can give yourself boils without the doctor noticing that you have "made" them yourself. All you need is a pin. Take the pin and scratch some film off your teeth. Then prick yourself with the infected pin in the leg or the arm, it doesn't matter where, until the place is bleeding. That's all. A few days later you'll have the finest and biggest boil in the world and you'll be able to stay in the hut for days; a boil shows, exhaustion doesn't – do you understand? Or if you want to get into the hospital hut, just drink an infusion of machorka. It'll be devastating, but very effective. You vomit, get diarrhoea and a high temperature.'

'Have you tried these things out yourself?'

'Of course I have, otherwise I would no longer be here.'

She also told me what can be done with a syringe and some milk. However, this 'procedure' is rather dangerous. We tried it out once later on. In the course of the ten years I had at least a dozen boils. Whenever I just could not carry on any longer, boils suddenly appeared on my body. It never occurred to any doctor that these boils were 'self-induced' which meant I could always stay in the hut for a few days.

'Another thing: always do the opposite of what the doctor tells you; if you are prescribed hot compresses, make cold ones, and vice versa. Do you understand?'

I understood at once and was a very conscientious pupil. The proof of this is that when I jammed my little finger in a door, I managed to stay in the hut for over a month; I had been prescribed warm compresses, and I stuck my finger in the snow.

'Why are you actually here? What sort of crime could you possibly have committed?' Valentina repeatedly asked me.

'At least I know what I'm in for, but you?' she continued.

In fact she was one of the very few Russian women whom I met in the course of the ten years who knew the reason for her imprisonment; she had belonged to an anti-Soviet group. She went on: 'Whatever were you Germans doing? After the occupation of the Ukraine and the advance into Russia you held all the trump cards. But instead of treating the people well and winning them over to your side, you did the opposite; you filled them with fear and terror. You deported them, tortured them and shot them. You were no better than the Soviets before you. And we were so longing for you to come. The people weep here, there, everywhere.'

What bitterness and disillusionment these sombre words revealed. It was not easy to explain to her that such disillusionment was inevitable. We went on discussing the subject whole nights through.

Weeks passed. I still had a high temperature. As did Valia. That was quite a simple matter; among the eleven patients in our room there were always several with high temperatures who every morning and evening when temperatures were being taken would stick several thermometers under their armpits and give them back to us before the nurse came.

'How high is your temperature to be this evening, Valia?'

'It had better be a bit higher than yesterday, 38.5°C perhaps.'

'And you, Emochka, what's yours to be today?'

'I don't want to have a temperature at all today; I've got to go to Vanya. He hasn't been to see me for quite a while; I daren't have a temperature any longer!'

'You are quite right,' said Valia, 'don't let your place be taken by that other woman.'

That evening for the first time in months I went into the laundry and bath hut. And there she was, the other woman, sitting in my place, by Ivan. I did not mind her sitting by him, but I did resent the way she was sitting there, and laughing and eating out of the same dish. That was going too far. They could sleep together if they wanted to, but as for her taking my rightful place, no, certainly not! How mockingly the two of them laughed when they saw me standing there with a blanket over my head and shoulders, my pyjama trousers showing below, and my over-large felt boots.

I was standing near to the big stove on which irons were put to heat. Slowly I took one in my hand, swung it this way and that, and approached this arrogant laughing hussy. She looked at me, then at the iron, and stopped laughing.

'You can see me, so stop it. Get out and don't come back!' I shouted at her and swung the hot iron to and fro in front of her terrified face.

'What do you want then? All right. I'm going. But I haven't done anything. Have I, Ivan?'

Ivan, glad that I had taken the matter in hand, kept quiet. The other woman hastily left the laundry room and told everyone how dangerous it was to start anything with Ivan Ivanovich; you ran the risk of being struck by his woman with a hot iron.

Then it was my turn to laugh!

When I was finally released from the hospital ward, Vanya could not immediately accommodate me in the laundry. But thanks to his connections, I obtained a post: as 'housekeeper' in the woman's hut. The morning started with fetching water – six wooden buckets each holding ten litres – then chopping wood and heating the metal stove. When all the women had left the hut, the scrubbing started; I took a fine wire coil and scraped it on the wooden floor with my bare feet until the floor was almost white and my feet had been scratched to pieces by the fine wire. Then the dirty water had to be carried out and poured away a long way behind the hut; there was wood to be sawn and chopped, so that the stove would not go out. After that there was water to be fetched again.

One day when I had just finished the morning scrubbing operation the camp leader entered with several officers.

'How many are you here?' one of them asked.

'Twenty-two women. Fifteen of them are working, three are sick and four on nightshift.'

'Your name and first name?'

'Goldacker, Emma Pavlovna.'

'Paragraph and sentence?'

'58/6. Ten years.'

The officer turned round angrily to the camp leader and spoke hectoringly: 'How is it possible for this woman to be working here inside the camp? A political prisoner! A German! And such light work! Get her out of this warm, clean hut! General labouring for her, in the tundra, or building work, or laying the railway track. It doesn't matter where, but just get her outside!'

The next morning I left the camp together with a brigade of men. I went into the forest for tree-felling; we laid railway lines; they sent me on building work, then back into the forest. And when summer came, hay-making started in the tundra.

When I heard in the evening that on the next day I was going hay-making with the men's brigade, I was very enthusiastic. Magnificent! Hay-making was not hard work. I had occasionally helped with hay-making as a young girl, and I clearly remembered how much I had enjoyed it. The next morning I set out, carefree and light-hearted, humming gently: 'Go out, my heart, and seek joy,' another Paul Gerhardt song that I had learned at school. I was glad to be alive and went out into the summer morning as if we were going on holiday. I had no awareness of what a playground the summer tundra is for countless tiny flies and midges – which penetrate eyes, nose, mouth and ears, and every tight space between clothes and body. I swallowed them as I breathed, and they sucked my blood. When I came back into the hut, I could scarcely keep my swollen eyes open. And next morning we had to go out again. The men's faces too were swollen beyond recognition.

They were all very kind to me. They had noticed on the first day that I had never held a scythe so they mowed my share.

'You know, you can look for mushrooms for us, if you like.'

'Mushrooms?' I replied, 'I only know chanterelles and the edible mushrooms which grow around Berlin.'

'Up here you needn't be afraid of poisonous toadstools; you take whatever you can find. They are all edible.'

'Is that true?'

'Yes, of course it is.'

'Good.' I answered, without conviction. Even so I went in search of these curious non-poisonous fungi and I certainly found them, gigantic magnificent looking fungi, all full of water – hardly surprising, up there in the sodden tundra. And I found vast quantities of yellow berries, something like blackberries, or bilberries but as big as cherries, really fine specimens – full of water, flavourless.

Later on when we sat round the fire, which we had stoked up with damp wood so that the smoke would keep away the flies, we divided my harvest. On the first evening I gave my share to a pregnant woman who had a craving for mushrooms. She gave me some butter in exchange (expectant mothers were given rations of butter and milk from the third or fourth month on). The next morning the woman who had eaten my fungi so ravenously was still alive, laughing and in the best of health. The men with whom I worked also showed no symptoms of poisoning at all. The next mushrooms I ate myself; and I had some butter into the bargain!

That September day, the eleven men and I were still hay-making. We still had swellings all over our bodies from the insect bites. And in spite of the supplements to our diet – in the form of fungi and berries – we were still hungry. As soon as we had arrived at our place of work, I left my men's brigade to look for fungi and berries, just as I did every other morning.

I strolled off, carrying my bag which held a piece of dry bread, some machorka and paper, two matches and a piece of the striking surface of a matchbox. I was not usually so well prepared for a long day out of doors; a piece of bread was as great a rarity as the machorka and the paper. I walked with my head down, always on the look-out for fungi and berries. How many kilometres had I been already? The air was no longer as hot and steamy as in August, and the minute stinging flies had calmed down somewhat as well. I shivered in my light felt boots which were wet through.

'It's already quite late. Where can the men be? I can't hear the scythes any more,' I thought and abruptly stood still.

I was on my own in the tundra. The forest seemed a long way off behind, on the horizon. All around me was nothing but sodden, hostile tundra. How could I find my brigade again? What should I do? If I were simply to go forward, further and further into the tundra, I might come out of it alive. I still had a piece of dry bread. I had meant to eat it by the fire in the evening, before we set out on the long walk back to the camp. I could set fire to a piece of wadding from my jacket and then let it smoulder, using the one match I had carefully kept. How often had we done this to keep fire burning the whole day? I would be free. For how long? The native inhabitants knew the tundra well, traversing it as they did with their herds of reindeer. For every escaped prisoner whom they betrayed they received a reward of 50 roubles. In the morning, when we went out to work, these recaptured fugitives would be lying near to the great gate so that everyone could see what had happened to them, how they were covered with blood, their skulls battered. But they had died free.

Should I go on? Just to die? To be put down like a sick dog? Where should I go? The damp September air already smelt of snow.

I shouted and whistled as loudly as I could. I stood still and hoped that I should be found before nightfall, so that I could have my evening soup together with my friends in the warm hut, so that I could put my wet shoes to dry out, so that I could go on living this life that I loved so much, this life that seemed so degrading. I whistled and shouted more and more loudly. Then, at last, I saw our guard, a small figure on the horizon. I ran towards him as quickly as I could, and would happily have thrown my arms around him. He did not give me the impression that he shared my joy. Quite the contrary!

He went for me. 'Stupid tart! I've been searching for you for hours, and now that I've found you – at last – I don't know where the men are.'

'Can't you hear? It's a train whistling. When I last saw the men they were near the railway line.'

'They are still there. At least I hope so. Hurry up. Come along now.'

'Wait for me, I can't jump over this wide stream, and I can't wade through it because I don't have gum boots, unlike you! Won't you help me?'

'What next? Do you expect me to carry you over perhaps?'

'That's just what I was thinking, that will be the quickest. You're the one in a hurry, not me!'

And he did carry me over the stream! I found it difficult not to laugh.

The men were waiting for us; they were visibly pleased to see their guard and me once more. We made our way back together, like sheep back to the fold. The train which had shown us the direction only passed every other day. It stopped near the coal pits where prisoners loaded it up with coal. Frequently, after the departure of the train the number of the convicts did not tally: another suicide. But the train had saved my life.

At last I was working in the warm again. Ivan Ivanovich had managed to wangle me a way out of the men's brigade and into the laundry. For nearly a year I had worked outside, day after day.

'Have you heard the latest, Ivan?' Vasili asked.

'No, and what's that? Don't tell me you've got your pockets full of machorka and you are hanging on to it!'

'Don't talk nonsense. This is really serious. The politicals are to be shoved off to Novaya Zemlya and put in chains there.'

'You're crazy, you've got it all wrong again; the criminal prisoners are being released, and just the politicals are staying in the camps in Inta.'

'That's not right. The politicals are getting chains on their feet. That's for sure, and your wife will be sent off and put in chains like all the others.'

'Shut up, idiot, I don't believe a word. Haven't you seen how they're rebuilding OP?'

'Yes, and I've heard that what they are doing in OP is for us as well,' I said, intervening in the conversation. I heard the tail end of the conversation just as I entered the ironing room, where the two men sat on the ironing table swinging their legs and smoking a roll-up together.

Every day new rumours circulated; and each day the conviction grew stronger that we were on the brink of a decisive change in our camp life. In OP, new huts were being built, as we had been able to see for a long time now from our camp; inside the new camp itself three huts set somewhat apart and surrounded by a fence could clearly be seen.

'That's the new women's camp,' Vasili could not restrain himself from commenting. It obviously gave him great pleasure to disturb us with this bad news.

'What does that matter? We can talk to each other through the fence. Can't we, Vanya?'

'Who's been telling you that I shall go marching off with the politicals?'

'What? You've always told me that you were a political as well.'

'Yes, of course, I've said so, but you see ...'

He became involved in a cock-and-bull story that just went on and on and which I finally interrupted with loud laughter. I had suspected his political paragraph for a long time; the speed and dexterity of his thefts and petty deceptions were far beyond the skill of a mere 'political'.

'Are you angry with me, Emochka?'

'No, not at all. What difference does it make?'

'Will you leave your ring here with me if you are sent away?'

'My ring? No, never. It belongs to me, and it always will belong to me.'

Ivan had begged me for the ring before, many times. He knew nothing about Serge. I had been careful never to mention anything about the relationship to him, but Ivan felt instinctively that this ring meant more to me than anything in the world. Once he had tried to strike a bargain: 'You wear it for one week, and then let me have it for a week. Do you agree?'

'No, Vanya. I shall never let it go, not even for a week.'

Vanya brought me a suitcase (a stolen one?) – a black wooden case. The inside of the lid bore the following inscription in his handwriting: 'Shestakova Emma Pavlovna.' Thus he gave me his name. Beneath it was written:

'I shall always wait for you.'

'Thank you, Vanya. Goodbye!'

'Goodbye, Emochka! But do let me have your ring, please.'

'No. Never. You know this very well. Goodbye.'

We stood there, ready to leave the long familiar camp and to go through the big gateway. As usual, the men had been led out before us women, and were waiting outside, well-guarded by dogs and soldiers. We were called out by name, and when the last of us had replied 'Here', the great gateway was opened once again. We pushed our way through, and the Sangorodok gate was closed behind us.

We moved slowly towards the reconstructed OP camp.

'So it's true then. The new buildings over there in OP were for us politicals,' Eva said.

I did not reply. I was thinking of Ivan Ivanovich. 'How strange!' I thought, 'Not very long ago – when we first talked about this separation – I was happy to think that I should finally be separated from this man, that I should not have to fight with him any more, to be rid of him for ever. And now?'

In the distance we saw the new fence around OP: the old wooden fence had been replaced by two rows of barbed wire three metres apart.

'Like a Nazi concentration camp,' I thought.

And then: 'Perhaps this fence is electrified.'

'Oh, no, surely not. That would make it too easy for politicals to commit suicide.'

We halted in front of the new camp. The march there had not lasted long at all, but we had to wait an endless time by the gateway until all the men had been thoroughly searched.

'They will take away everything that we have. We shall be left with empty suitcases!' said Ira, the Leningrad teacher.

I thought anxiously of all the valuable things held by my wooden case: my blue and white checked dress with the belt that was so brightly coloured and so carefully plaited together; my knitting needles – what precious objects they were! – I had made them myself out of stiff wire, and they would be very difficult to replace; yes, and then my toothbrush, found while street-sweeping in Inta – it was to be in fact the only toothbrush that I was to possess during my ten years' imprisonment; and then – most precious of all – the large piece of soap, washing soap, which had obviously come from the washhouse.

'On no account can that soap be found. I can't do that to Vanya! Two boys aged fourteen and fifteen had been sentenced to fifteen years in a labour camp because of a kilogram of potatoes stolen from the collective farm! A piece of soap of this size would get me at least ten years, if not more. My suitcase must not be opened.'

I stood in the last row of the column of women. The first women were already being searched. I took my case and went slowly towards the front where I could help the women whose cases had already been searched as they collected up their things that had been strewn around. Doing this, it was quite easy to put my case among those which had already been searched. I just needed to use the general confusion. Thanks to this trick, I moved into OP, once a convalescent camp now a special camp for political prisoners, without being parted from a single treasure, and without compromising Vanya.

Vasili was proved right; the three huts fenced in within the camp were for us women. Hundreds of women were already there when we arrived. There were only about twenty of us new arrivals, and space had to be made for us. To right and left, and along the hut walls of the third hut, there were two shelves of planks which had already been claimed by other women. Shouts, curses and blows greeted us.

'You there in front on the right, make room, if you please. You can easily move closer together. You are not nearly as close as you might be!' the woman guard shouted to us, before locking the hut door from the outside.

They did in fact make a little space for us at the front on the right, just near the entrance, on the upper and lower shelves, just enough for us to lie down – not on our backs certainly, but at least on our sides. We all went to sleep on our right sides, and then at night with one accord we turned over on to the left. In this way we avoided breathing into each others' faces. As in prison, the inevitable bucket stood in a corner close to the exit. Anyone unfortunate enough to have to make use of it at night would lose her sleeping place and be forced to lie on the cold floor for the rest of the night.

In the morning the usual cabbage soup was doled out, together with a piece of bread – damp, black bread. Only then was the door to the hut opened. We had to go out to work – men's work, building work.

We had to prepare the beams that were needed for building; tree trunks had their bark removed and were transported from place to place. At midday, soup was brought to where we worked, along with four and a half spoonfuls of mash, made with no fat and often with no salt either. In the evening back at the camp there would be nothing more to eat. Nothing. There was nothing except the stinking, locked hut, nothing except intolerable noise and incessant cursing. The sick were carried off into another hut. Natural selection? Or simply negligence?

When I shut my eyes I saw the most varied pictures pass by me at furious speed, as if I were in a film: houses in the country; gardens behind whose fences stood large sunflowers; ripening, billowing cornfields with large red poppies; then the sea, and again cornfields; then again displays of food in big stores. I ran through burning streets and saw once more the van full of corpses in the train.

'This must be what it's like when you go mad,' I thought.

I was afraid to close my eyes. It started again every evening. Then day broke once more, the soup was brought in and men's work went on.

'Hello, German woman, come over here.' The man who brought the tools to our workplace whispered to me unobtrusively.' Take this axe here. It has a particularly good cutting edge.'

'Thank you,' I said taking the axe. I replied to his winking with a slight nod.

I had understood him at once and scratched away the earth from the axe without being noticed. A letter from Vanya. It had been folded up small, no bigger than a postage stamp. A letter from Sangorodok, a letter which came to me in this camp of slaves, from life outside, a letter indicating that somebody was still thinking of me in the almost free world – for that was how Sangorodok seemed to me. Vanya had not forgotten me. It was dangerous for him to write to me, a political prisoner. He had done so in spite of the risk. I was happy. Sangorodok, the years with Vanya – could a foreign woman prisoner expect more?

Vanya kept on writing to me, humorous, witty letters. A cat had attached itself to him: 'I've called it "Emochka",' he wrote on one occasion. Throughout a whole long day I smiled whenever I thought of it. Later on he even found a way of sending me a tin full of margarine. On the tin, he had used a nail to scratch Constantine Simonov's words to the actress Serova: 'Wait for me as I wait for you, Vanya.'

I wanted to please him too, truly to give him joy. How often had he begged me for the ring? I sewed the ring into a tiny letter that had been folded flat and which I had stuck on to the axe with loam, following his example. Did I really want him to get that ring? Being superstitious like the people around me, I secretly thought and hoped that the ring would be brought back: it had always been returned to me before.

The first time had been in Berlin when the officer had stared at my dirty hands and had not noticed the ring; then later, in the Frankfurt prison, the drunken soldier had torn the ring from me, and had not the Russian woman to whom he had given it, handed it back to me the next day? In the railway van I had tried to barter the ring for bread, as I had already bartered the gold coins. The soldier kept my ring for two days before giving it back to me, saying contemptuously: 'Nobody wants to exchange anything for that tin thing. They all want gold.' Even in Inta, that was true. Once, during the time I was working with the men's brigade, we had made a fire at the edge of the tundra to thaw out our bread. I had held my frozen fingers over the fire for a long time. I was just about to spear a piece of bread with a twig so that I could hold it over the fire, when Mitya threw me backwards into the snow. While he pressed my shoulders into the snow, his friend Kostya tore the ring off my finger.

I begged them both: 'Leave me my ring. It's got no value. Give it back to me. It's only base metal. Give me my ring! My only souvenir of home!'

At first I shouted, and they made fun of me; then I implored them, and they laughed out loud. Mitya and Kostya kept my ring. I wept – not only on account of the lost ring, but because they had laughed at me. When three days later a very friendly supervisor, for whom I had been waiting, came on duty, I asked him: 'Can you do something for me?'

'It all depends on what you want from me.'

'Well, Mr Prosvetov, Kostya and Mitya have stolen my ring. It has absolutely no value, but it means a great deal to me. Could you please try to bring me back my ring? They live in the fourteenth hut.'

'Hmm.'

'Yes, yes, I know that I'm not entitled to wear any ornaments, and I promise that if you bring it back to me, I will take it straight away to the clothing storeroom. But please do this for me.'

He left; I waited impatiently for him in the women's hut; I was sitting on my plank bed when he entered, his good-natured face beaming. 'Here, have your ring back again, but I don't want to see it on you ever again. Do you understand?'

'Oh, thank you. Thank you!'

I hid the ring – at least for a short time.

'I expect my ring will come back to me all the same,' I thought when I sent it off.

It did not come back. Vanya received it and kept it. That was in November 1948.

Six years later I met Ivan Ivanovich once more in Inta. I was one of a group of women clearing dirty snow from one of Inta's many streets, a street we had helped to build earlier on. Our working area was cordoned off with a thick rope, meant to stop contact between free people and prisoners. Suddenly I recognized Ivan Ivanovich walking along the road scrutinizing the women at work there. He saw me and recognized me at once. He was a free man. He approached our supervisor, gave him a banknote (that sort of thing was quite possible) and gained permission to talk to me. The supervisor called me over. Vanya and I stood facing one another after all those years.

'When will you be set free?' was his first question.

'Next year.'

'Oh yes? You always told me that you would be set free by 1954.'

'No, Vanya, you're wrong there,' I replied.

I glanced at his hands. I saw my ring on the little finger of his left hand and I begged him: 'Give me my ring back. You know very well what it means to me.'

'Niet, Emochka. I'm keeping the ring. As long as I've got it, I know that you will come to me when you're set free. If I were to give it to you today, I know that I should never see you again!'

I turned away from him and took my spade in my hand again. He wrote to me once or twice more, for he knew now which camp I was in. I never replied.

That was all over.

Ivan Ivanovich died in 1957. He had my ring on his little finger. Nobody could take it off; it would have had to be removed with a saw.

6

At the end of November we were transferred to yet another camp. It was also in Inta, but, as it was a long way from OP, we were loaded on to a coal train made up of open trucks. This short journey might have been quite enjoyable in fact, if it had not been so icily cold. In the early morning the thermometer registered -40°C. These small, moving trucks where we were pressed close together, the continued waiting, the jacket which offered scarcely any warmth (I had already pulled out too much wadding at monthly intervals, to deal with menstruation), the small scrap of bread which never satisfied our hunger; it was not surprising that I stared ahead of me hungry, frozen and sad.

When we finally arrived at our new camp in the afternoon, I was completely apathetic. I did not want to quarrel and fight in order to get hold of a more or less satisfactory place on a plank bed of 60 centimetres or less in width. It was always the same: you had to be the first if you wanted a good place to sleep; the first if it was a question of getting a larger piece of bread than your neighbour; the first if you wanted a large ration of kasha; the first, the first. What the hell did it all matter? I was fed up with having to struggle for every tiny advantage, so instead of hurrying or even racing as usual, as soon as we came into the camp, I slowed down. Let the rest of them run. There would be a place for me; it did not matter what it was like. The first hut that I tried was already over full, as was the second. The third smelt of children's nappies and milk that had boiled over. Mothers and small children were shouting and crying. No thank you, that would not suit me, even if there were a free place there. I went straight out again, without even asking. I would find something all right. The fourth hut was even more overcrowded than the first. And so it went on.

Ivan's suitcase became heavier and heavier; I could scarcely drag it along any more.

'I've had bad luck this time, I shan't find any sleeping place tonight. The best I can hope for is the floor at the entrance to a hut.'

I came to the twelfth hut. Crowded out! I knew before I went in. I was at the end of my tether.

'Can you possibly find room for me?' I turned to the senior person of the hut, convinced that the answer would be no.

Then my glance fell upon a tiny grey and black green-eyed cat.

I could not help thinking of Vanya and his cat, and I started to talk in German to the tiny cat: 'Come along then, pussy, come and be stroked. Come on.'

I cannot remember what else I said. I only know that my despondent mood disappeared instantly. The senior person of the hut, whom I had not noticed at all at first, looked at me with large, surprised blue eyes and spoke in fluent German: 'You're German, aren't you? Can I talk German to you?'

'Yes, of course. And what about you?'

'Me? I was born here in Russia, but my parents are German, You must be looking for a place to sleep. Will you have mine? I work at night and sleep in the daytime, so you can have my place for the night. Is that alright?'

'You will do this for me? Thank you, thank you very much!'

I had known all along that I should find a place in spite of everything!

The next morning we started work setting up a new fence round the camp. As in OP, two barbed-wire barriers had to be fixed about three metres apart; this was to replace the high wooden fence. First of all deep holes had to be dug for the posts; a post was rammed in every three metres, then the lengths of barbed wire were put in place. Fortunately, our camp was fairly small, so that we finished this unpleasant work quite quickly. There were about 45–50°C of frost; in this bitterly cold weather all the other women stayed in their huts. Normally outside work stopped when the temperature sank to −42°C, but we newcomers had to work outside in spite of the cold until the barbed-wire fence was constructed.

The fence was finished, the intense cold persisted, and, at last, we too were able to stay in our hut. For a week not a single work party left the camp, not even the firewood brigade, and this meant that the huts could no longer be heated. One day without a fire in the stove was just tolerable, but by the second day the cold in the hut was unendurable.

'Something will have to be done about this,' I said to myself and called to Agnes.

'Look, Agnes, there's a big post lying in the 'no-man's land' between the two rows of barbed wire. I could not be bothered to drag it away. But I still know where it is.'

'What about it?'

'It's obvious: we should go and fetch it for firewood.'

'Good. Let's go.'

We found the place where the post was quite easily. It was so cold that we were more or less hidden in a fog of minute ice particles.

'I don't think we can be seen from the watchtower.'

'Definitely not,with this fog!' Agnes said.

'Stay behind me. I'll try to pull the post into the camp.'

As agreed, Agnes remained behind me, and, disregarding the prohibition on being within three metres of the barbed-wire fence, I bent right over and crept close up to it.

'Damn! I can't reach the post from here. It's further outside than I thought.'

There was nothing for it, if I wanted a warm hut, but to force my way through the barbed wire, first putting my right leg cautiously through, then, still bent over, drawing my right arm and the top part of my body carefully through next. I had soon grabbed hold of the post.

'I've got it, Agnes,' I just had time to say before a bullet whizzed past, just missing my head.

'Hell, they've seen us,' I swore, but I did not let go of the post once I had taken hold of it; I shoved it through the barbed wire into the camp area, made my way back afterwards, and with the post over my shoulder hurried back into the hut. After this, illicitly sawing and chopping up the wood presented barely any problem, and soon a magnificent fire crackled in our stove.

But, 'What's that strange noise outside?'

'Come on, Agnes. Let's go and see what's happening!'

We soon discovered the reason for the noise; the shot from the watchtower had woken up the camp officers, who were standing at the scene of our 'theft'. Innocently, Agnes asked: 'Whoever can have been trying to escape when it's as cold as this?'

'Quiet! Be quiet, can't you? I want to speak now. That goes for you in your corner back there as well!'

The Naryadshitza[4] was attempting to make herself heard amid the shouting that was usual in our hut.

'Do just be quiet!'

At the third attempt she finally made herself heard above the noise.

'Now listen. I need a woman for the washhouse. From three or four o'clock in the morning until ten or eleven at night. It's a job in the warm! Any volunteers? It's for the new nursery!'

Nobody stirred.

'How about you, fascist, don't you want to volunteer?'

The 'fascist' was me.

'Well, why not? It's all right with me.'

'You must be completely mad,' Agnes said.

'No, not at all. You'll soon see; if I am to do the laundry, I shall get soap, and with soap quite a lot of other things can be gained.'

'But you can't possibly work for twenty hours a day, it's just not possible.'

'Oh, I'm sure it's only like that at first. I'll manage it all right.'

I went behind the Naryadshitza to the nursery. Presumably I was the only volunteer because it was shortly before Christmas, and the others did not want to have their festivities spoiled by a never-ending job like this.

'Here's your washerwoman, Sophia Michailovna. She can begin at once.'

Sophia – before her arrest she had probably been the youngest lecturer in political economics at Leningrad University – piled a gigantic bundle of dirty washing on my back. 'A hundred and sixty nappies, sixty sheets. When you've finished with this lot, come back to me to fetch the next bundle.'

'Good.'

When I passed the hospital hut with my load on my back, I had a quick look at the thermometer: –41°C, no wonder that I could no longer feel my hands. In my hurry I had left my gloves in the hut. Fortunately it was not far to the washhouse. A cloud of steam enveloped me as I entered.

[4] A prisoner who is responsible for the allocation of work.

'Shut the door, you filthy German. We've had your sort here long enough. Get out!'

What a warm welcome! But I could not expect a better one. I tried to be fair-minded; these Russian and Ukrainian women had all had direct experience of the war. Their hostility should not surprise me, for they knew nothing of my background, after all. It was not their concern; I could understand them. 'The people weep here and there, the people weep everywhere,' Valentina Semionovna had said.

They carried on abusing me. What a good thing it was that Valentina had taught me how to defend myself.

'I need a couple of wash tubs. Give me them now! These are mine. And nobody had better come near me!' I yelled out fluently and aggressively above their insults.

Two of the washerwomen laughed; the others cursed and called me a dirty German woman, and more. Meanwhile I took possession of two tubs and a corner of the washhouse, by the side of the big boilers. In 'life as it was before' – this was the way we used to describe our past – I had hardly ever had an opportunity to do washing on a large scale. But I just had to cope with it, if I wanted to keep the job. As in the past, washing was done on a washing board, which was hard work, but all the same, less of a strain than working with pickaxe and spade outside in the freezing cold. Of course it was best to accept this place in the warmth, I continually told myself as I washed mountains of nappies and sheets. Then as one of the washerwomen approached my wash tub: 'Get away from here. This is my place. Do you understand?'

'Hold your trap, you Fascist whore. I do as I please here. The times when you lot gave the orders are finished!' She came closer and closer to my place and did not stop jeering at me. If she succeeded in stealing just one of my nappies, I could lose my job. I happened to have a wet, dirty nappy in my hand. A split second later she had it in her face. Angrily she threw herself upon me. We slipped on the soapy floor of the washhouse. Being smaller and quicker than she was, I succeeded in freeing myself from her, and with both hands I pressed on her throat.

The others poured cold water on us, and we got up again.

'You didn't do so badly, you filthy German,' Shura, the thief, said.

After that, she defended me through thick and thin. Soon I no longer had to wash merely nappies and children's sheets. My tasks included washing the white overalls worn by the nurses and the staff of the children's kitchen.

'Have a look in my overall pocket,' Nastya, the Finnish cook, whispered to me one morning as I was fetching the kitchen washing. I found wrapped in her overall a piece of bread. No, not a piece, a whole loaf. A kilogram of bread, damp, black bread, but nonetheless bread.

'Agnes, Agnes, are you asleep?'

'No, what is it?'

'Nothing special. Are you hungry?'

'What a stupid question. I'm always hungry!'

I then drew the big, black loaf slowly and cautiously out of the sleeve of my jacket. We finished it in one night and wept as we ate. We wept for joy. It was years since we had seen a whole loaf of bread.

Nastya kept on giving us more help. Whenever she could, she hid some food in her overall. Sometimes it would be sugar, at another time a piece of butter or bacon, or some peeled potatoes, but most frequently bread.

'You see, Agnes, people who have soap have a lot of other things too!'

'True enough, but have you had a look at your hands?'

'That doesn't matter at all. The main thing is that we have got something to eat!'

'Here, Marlene, take the washing to be dried. We shall get a piece of bacon for this!'

Marlene, who was heating the big cauldrons for the bath, hung the washing which I gave her at the back of her big store to dry. I did some washing for Russian prisoners who did not want their laundry handled in the general washhouse and who because of their parcels could afford to have their things washed privately. In this way I became the 'private washerwoman'.

'It's three o'clock already! Quick, get up, you must go and make the deliveries!'

Marlene shook me until I woke up, and showed me the huge pile of cleanly ironed laundry which she had brought into the hut for me on a board. I jumped up quickly from the plank bed and took the clean washing to its owners. I had to be finished with the delivery before the general wake-up call, since it was absolutely essential not to be seen doing this work.

'Marussya, quick, take your laundry!'

'What's the matter?'

'Your laundry, quick, put it away!'

She took the clean washing sleepily and gave me a bag full of sugar.

'Tanya, here are your vests. Do you hear?'

'Yes, yes. Here is some dried fruit from the Caucasus!'

A third woman gave me margarine. On the evening of such 'delivery days', as we called them, our little group would all sit together in one of the huts, enjoying all the good things our washing had brought us.

'Do you see, Agnes, how right I was?'

Agnes smiled without replying.

I used to work for eighteen to twenty hours a day (later on, the hours were reduced to fourteen to sixteen). Even so, this work in the washhouse was designated 'light work', since it meant staying in the camp and avoided being outside in the cold day after day. To ensure that my place in warm quarters was handed over to other people from time to time, I could never work in the wash house for longer than a few months, or at most a year. After that time, I had to go out into the cold and snow again. Because of this, I found myself in a brigade which was ordered every day to do general work outside the camp. Every morning we put kilometre after kilometre behind us before reaching our work place on the edge of the tundra. I was already tired and exhausted before the day's work began. We were digging ditches through the tundra. With every step I sank deep into the snow, often right up to my hips. My felt boot would get stuck in the snow. While one girl tried to pull the boot out of the snow again, another massaged my naked foot in order to prevent frostbite.

Sometimes I was unable to remove my hands from the spade any more, cramped and frozen as they were. Towards six o'clock in the evening we came back to the camp; we had spent twelve hours without a break in the cold. Our reward for this consisted of a bowl of cabbage soup and a piece of bread in the morning and in the evening cabbage soup again, four and a half spoonfuls of gruel, the so-called 'kasha', and bread, three hundred grams of black, soggy bread; if we had worked well, somewhat more! Sometimes there was a piece of fish; or on great national holidays such as 1 and 2 January or 7 and 8 November we would be rewarded with a piece of meat. It seemed that this was enough.

We marched in long columns, five linking arms together. In this way two out of the five could sleep as they marched. The other three led and supported them. When you have got the hang of it, it is possible to sleep quite well like this. It was my turn and I was sleeping so soundly, that I felt I had slept for hours. My neighbour woke me roughly: 'Don't you have something to hide? Hurry up, we are almost there!'

I had half a pound of margarine with me; a former prisoner had obtained it for me in Inta. Over my left arm I was carrying the thick stockings which we put on when we wore gum boots. Without thinking about it for long and being still half asleep, I slipped the margarine from my jacket pocket into one of the stockings.

'With a bit of luck I shall get through,' I thought, 'perhaps they will only do a quick search.'

On the contrary. They made a thorough search.

It began badly; five women supervisors positioned themselves in front of the first row of five, so that there was one supervisor for each prisoner. Where could I hide my margarine in a hurry? I simply had to get it through. I had been looking forward so much to presenting my 'little family', that is, my friends, with bread with margarine on it that evening. Soon it was our turn. The gateway was wide open as the first row had already been admitted into the camp. Without further thought I rushed past my supervisor, through the gateway and straight towards the huts. My supervisor tried to catch me up, but I had a slight start. I turned round the corner of a hut and bumped into another supervisor; at the moment of impact I just had time to drop my thick stockings with the precious margarine behind the water butt at the corner of the hut. As I had hidden my margarine, I now allowed myself to be searched without resistance. She did not find anything and took me to the camp officer.

'What had you got to hide? Why did you run away?'

'Oh, I only wanted to be first in the hut so that I could get enough water to be able to wash myself thoroughly'.

He turned to the supervisor: 'Put her in the lockup for five days, but don't allow her to wash.'

The supervisor brought me into the lockup without letting me go first into the dining room. On the way we met Anna: 'Behind the water butt by the twelfth hut. The margarine is in my thick stockings. Fetch them quickly!' I whispered in German as I passed her.

Anna had understood. It did not matter to me now that I was to be locked up. The lockup had a very high ceiling, no heat, no window, no bed. A board that was tipped up and supported at one end served as a bed at night, when the supervisor gave the prisoner the second support. In the lockup corridor I had to strip down to my vest. At night I was handed, along with the bed support, my jacket to use as a cover. Outside it was 38°C below zero. As in prison the inmates of the lockup were given gruel only every other day. On the day when there was no soup there was not even a piece of bread. Nothing. You either gave up the ghost or survived.

Prisoners in the lockup were often sent out to work. Without any more food, of course. The task was to clean out the soldiers' latrines. I refused and, miracle of miracles, was not given an extra punishment. The next day, in the lockup cell, the Judas window in the cell door was pushed open, something fell on to the floor and the window was closed again immediately. I was sitting in a squatting position on my heels, close to the door to the corridor. This was the warmest place. Without getting up I could feel over the floor of the cell; the little packet was soon in my hands. Even before I had removed the paper, I could recognize the contents by the smell; a piece of sausage, garlic sausage. How lovely life could be! I had hardly got it down when the window opened again and once more something fell down to the ground. Incredible! This time it was bread and margarine – four double slices spread thickly with margarine. I still had the taste of the sausage in my mouth and now proceeded to enjoy the sandwiches.

'Now I only need a cigarette to be completely happy,' I thought, replete in a good mood, and already ambitiously demanding.

I had scarcely finished formulating this thought when the window opened a third time and a tiny package fell directly at my feet – three half cigarettes, a few matches and a small piece of emery paper. With such provisions, I could survive the hunger and cold of the remaining days in the lockup. When I was released, I was unsteady on my feet, but Anna called to fetch me and supported me. It was she who had smuggled the little packages into the lockup for me.

'How lovely that girl is over there,' I thought admiringly, as I arranged myself on my plank bed in the new hut.

We had once again been transferred into a different hut. I knew nobody in the new hut, and as I had nothing else to do, I went on staring at the beautiful girl who was sprawling on the bed and stretching herself like a cat.

'Marina, are you coming into the dining room with me?' a girl said to her as she was passing.

'No, but do please bring me my kasha when you come back. You can eat the soup yourself. All right?'

She was called Marina and she did not want to go for her food. Was she ill? She did not seem sick. I could not keep my eyes off her. Our eyes met.

'No!' I fought against myself. 'That's how it begins. Is it really happening to me too? No, anything but that!'

I did not want to become one of those women who fell in love with a woman and then became involved in the worst scenes of jealousy; who wrestled or had knife fights over a woman – women fought about women – like Ivan who had once attacked the barber with a knife because he had tried to approach me. No, I didn't want that.

Everyone was in the canteen. Apart from us, the hut was empty. I had not noticed this. Marina was still lolling about on her plank bed. I felt compelled to look in her direction. Once more our eyes met. Nobody brought my kasha along to me, but that did not matter. I did not feel hungry.

When on the following day I came back from work to the hut, I only desired one thing, to be looking at Marina; I hoped that our eyes would meet again. I could see that she was expecting me. This time I was well aware that we were on our own in the hut, and I went over to her. This was what she had been waiting for.

'Good evening, Marina,' was all that I could say.

'Good evening.'

'Emma Pavlovna,' I added, introducing myself and taking the hand which she offered me.

How lovely she was! It was impossible not to fall in love with those dark-blue eyes. Never until then had I seen such beautiful eyes. And that ever-smiling, enchanting mouth!

'Are you ill?' I asked, simply in order to say something.

'No. I just don't want to go out. I can always find some girl who will bring me my kasha.'

'Uh huh!' was all I said, feeling a stab of jealousy.

She took hold of my hand. I stroked hers gently. My fingers touched her eyes, her lips.

'Hey! Marina! Here, you can have your kasha and your bread, but don't imagine that I shall ever bring anything to you again.'

It was the same girl who had brought the broth the previous evening. She looked at us with eyes full of hatred. I had just kissed Marina.

Days and weeks passed. There was snow. In order to be alone, we strolled arm in arm through the camp. We did not need words. Looks and gestures sufficed us. With my arm round her waist and her head on my shoulder, what a blissful feeling of inner warmth!

One day I realized I was tired of these pointless caresses. I went to Anna.

'Anna, listen. Will you come now and again in the evenings to see me in the hut a bit? I should like to talk to you.'

'Why? Is something special happening?'

'Actually, no. But you'll see. I've got to talk to you.'

Anna came. She listened to me, and even while I was talking to her, I was aware that the spell was broken: I could look across to Marina with quite a normal glance. It was true, she was as pretty as a picture, but how stupid she was basically!

The next day I ate my kasha again with a hearty appetite.

Later on, when we were in Abes where the Germans from all camps of 'Komi ASSR' were gathered before being repatriated, I received love letters from a woman; she made the craziest declarations of love. In order to nip the affair in the bud, I made fun of it in public. She soon got over it. I also recall a prostitute who occasionally had a lesbian relationship.

'It's all very well in its way,' she said, 'but it can't compare with having a man!'

Most homosexual couples were found amongst the women from Western Europe, especially intellectuals. The Russian women were less complicated in this respect, perhaps in a sense more 'normal'. It is true, there were Russian lesbians, but the relationship was all much more obvious, cruder, and less subtle. Nevertheless, during the final months in Russian camps the lesbian Western Europeans no longer restrained themselves. One could hear women addressing their 'men' by male first names, and see female couples in close embrace or exchanging passionate kisses.

7

After the great separation of political and criminal prisoners the former were forbidden to write letters freely; they were allowed to write only once a month. However, this applied only to Russian prisoners. Foreign prisoners were simply denied any right to have contacts outside the camp.

In Sangorodok I had exchanged my sugar ration for a piece of paper and a pencil; I had even got hold of stamps. Fortunately I did not need envelopes, as it was usual at that time in Russia to fold the letter when it was ready in the shape of a triangle – half of the rear side of the letter had to remain free – and then to address this triangle. I had often bartered my sugar and bread for this purpose. During the first years I wrote and sent off at least thirty of these triangular letters from Sangorodok – to my mother, to an aunt, and again to my mother. Each time I said to myself: 'This letter will surely arrive. It must. One day they are going to call out my name when the mail is being distributed!'

Finally the day came when my name really was called out. It was before we were separated from the criminal prisoners. Though had been waiting so long for the time when my name would be read out, when it happened I was terrified. I went very slowly towards the woman who was distributing the letters. She had not just one letter for me, but many, many letters. A whole package. They were my own letters which I had written full of hope during the last two and a half years. They had got no further than Moscow.

In order to protect my mother from being arrested as well, I had said during one of my first interrogations that I had no relatives in Berlin. That was noted in my file and was in effect a complete ban on my writing, since we were only allowed to write to immediate family. So I no longer needed to exchange my sugar and bread for paper or stamps. Two and a half years of hoping and waiting had been for nothing. For years I was unable to stay in the hut when the mail was being distributed. At first I put my head under the bed cover, but then I used to leave the hut. I could not bear to hear the names that were being read out nor the joyful cries of those who received post. I went outside into the cold or else into the drying room (which each hut had). I had worked just as hard as the Russian women; why did I not have the same rights as they did, these Russians who were in any case no better than I was? It did no good to fret. But many times I longed to weep, to cry out or to knock my head against the wall; I could have smashed everything up in impotent rage! Instead I left the hut with my head held high, not saying a word. Nobody saw me weeping.

In the drying room I would chat with the girl who happened to be on duty there until the distribution of the mail was over. This made waiting easier, and stopped me thinking of the letters I should never receive.

At the end of 1951 the Christmas mail was given out. In the drying room I could hear unusual shouts from the hut, then footsteps, laughter and calling.

'It's not true. I must be mistaken. It can't be my name which they keep on calling out.'

The door to the drying room was flung open. My name – this time I heard it loudly and clearly – was called out. An eternity passed before I was standing stiffly and rigidly in front of the Naryadshitza.

'Dance, dance!' she said to me, laughing.

I could neither dance nor speak; I stood before her motionless and silent. She held out a letter to me, a big fat letter.

'From my mother,' the idea flashed through my mind.

The letter was not from my mother, but from Valentina Simeonovna who had been released from the camp some months earlier. She had understood much better than anyone else how poor, wretched and unhappy we foreigners were. And she had written to me. A letter! A letter from freedom! She had enclosed with this letter more than a dozen photographs: of herself, of Tamara, her daughter from whom she had almost completely separated so that she could study – her daughter had still gone to her in Siberia and there they were in the pictures, the two of them, mother and daughter, radiant and laughing as they picked berries in the taiga – pictures of their new friends, former prisoners who were banished to Siberia after finishing their sentences. I just had to keep looking again at Tamara and Valentina. Tamara had been five years old when her mother was arrested. Now she was seventeen. How pleased I was for Valentina that her daughter had come to her in Siberia in spite of all the lies that had been told her about her mother. She had not forgotten her mother. Valentina wrote that Tamara was a member of the Komsomols, for after all, she did so much want to study! Tamara's father had been shot by the Soviets long before Valentina herself was arrested. I looked again and again at the pictures from the taiga: there they were again, mother and daughter; then the new friends, gathered at Valentina's around the richly laden Easter table; then again the two new friends, little old women; then Tamara alone with a little pig; then again Valentina on her own. She had written to me that I would receive a parcel, but not until the pig had been slaughtered. She kept her word.

I was the first German woman in the camp to receive a parcel. I took a childish delight in letting them all think that the parcel was from Germany. On one occasion Valentina sent me money; then another time bacon and clothing: a jacket, a bright-red knitted cardigan and a nightdress, the first nightdress that I had seen since my arrest, and what was more, it was my own! I had not seen anything like it for seven years. I put on the simple white nightdress, placed myself on my plank bed and summoned all my friends so that they could admire me in my finery. That evening was full of laughter.

Valentina did all this for me because she belonged to my little family with whom I had shared my bread, for whom I had done washing, for whom I had given German or English lessons, for whom I knitted and for whom – to my shame, let it be said – I had stolen now and again. In short, Valentina was a friend.

In February 1954, when my sentence was already drawing to its close, we were given double cards so that we could write to our relatives in Germany. Soviet Russia had joined the Red Cross and the Red Crescent. At last! But what is a card after nine years of silence? I no longer had any desire to write it. My mother was sure to have died, or if she were still alive, she would certainly have got used to the thought that I would not come back again. I did not want to have anything to do with 'life before'. I was also afraid of knowing that my mother was really dead. Finally my friends succeeded in persuading me to write. A month passed, and then double cards were distributed again. I had not had a reply to my first card. Each of us had to collect her card in person from the Political Officer who naturally took the opportunity to question us about our morale and that of our fellow prisoners. When I went to him and asked for my card, he explained to me that I was prohibited from writing, since my file contained the note: 'no relatives'. I had known this a long time, since that day on which all my triangular letters had come back to me from Moscow. So this revelation did not surprise me. I shrugged my shoulders and simply said: 'nothing doing, then,' and was about to go.

The officer called me back with a friendly smile. How I hated him! He suggested to me that I should hand in a petition to Moscow and give the name, address and nature of relationship of the person to whom I wanted to write. (Letters were still only allowed to direct relatives.) This request would not be refused me. I turned round on the sole of my foot and said curtly: 'It's almost ten years since I wrote, so I can continue doing without'.

I slammed the door behind me.

The repulsive-friendly words of the officer led me to conclude rapidly that my first card had been sent off and not yet come back. So there was still hope that I should receive a reply. It was not until the second cards were distributed that they had noticed that I had been prohibited from writing. Their slackness had been my opportunity. If the first card had actually reached my mother, she would not need a second one: she would know that I was alive. And if she were no longer alive and the card were sent back, why should I go on bended knees seeking for permission to write?

I learned later that my first card did arrive. It came on a Sunday morning. My mother had not been at home. Our neighbour who had taken in the card had a rough idea where she could find my mother and went right across Berlin in order to give her the card. In the end she found my mother at the home of a sister-in-law where the whole family were gathered to celebrate the confirmation of my cousin Knut.

In April 1954, two months after I had written my first card, I received the first parcel from my mother. It was a tiny package in comparison with the large parcels the others received. The reason for this was that I had written on my card that we were allowed to receive parcels of up to two kilograms. In fact, they could weigh up to four or five kilograms, but I did not know whether my mother could afford to send such a large parcel. On my card I had asked for photographs, and these would have to be sent in a package; only cards or parcels were allowed, no letters. In my mother's small parcel there was an envelope right at the top with the photographs I had asked for.

The parcels were handed out in the camp depot in the presence of an officer. A soldier opened the parcel, the officer inspected the contents. I immediately identified the package with my mother's handwriting on it. I stood in front of it as if rooted to the spot. The soldier opened the parcel; I could see the envelope which the officer took out first; then he looked at the pictures. I was able to glance swiftly at them from the side: it was my family, my mother, some children; they had to be my brother's children. He put the envelope with the pictures away and gave me the contents of the parcel, one item after another: cigarettes, honey, chocolate; there was even a tin of strawberries there!

Two days later I was given the photographs at long last. The officer said, as he gave them to me: 'It is good to see that somebody in your family is a member of the Komsomols.'

He showed me the picture of a young girl, undoubtedly my niece, who had a plain-coloured scarf round her neck. She certainly had nothing to do with the Communist youth movement, but he had assumed that she had, and that was the sole reason why he handed on the photographs so quickly.

I was overcome with joy. There was my family, my very own large family; there they all were around me arranged on my plank bed. I could no longer say a word. Stunned with happiness I kept looking at the pictures.

My mother, whose features had been gradually growing hazy in my memory, was there: plump and laughing, she was holding a large bunch of grapes in her hand. How could I ever have thought that she was dead? Naturally I immediately put in a petition and requested the 'high council' in Moscow for permission to write. As it happened, my mother's address had already been registered because of the parcel. There was nothing to hide any more.

A short time before I wrote the first card, I had stopped smoking. I was tired of the taste of machorka, of being dependent on tobacco, and determined to give it up. I was so much my own self that I did not want my feeling of inner freedom to be restricted by anything, not even by machorka!

But oh, how much I enjoyed the cigarettes from Germany, all the same!

Today they shot Galina. Why? Why not? They can do what they like with us. The soldier who shot her was rewarded with a special leave of absence and another medal on his uniform.

Galina was a young Pole. She had been arrested for giving a glass of water to a German soldier who passed by; she had been sentenced to ten years imprisonment. She was pregnant when she came into prison. A short time before her death, her five-year-old daughter Svetlana had been sent to an orphanage in the interior of Russia, far away from her mother who would never see her again. Galina was very quiet and reserved. No one ever heard her say much. She died as quietly as she had lived. Like all the women that day, she was collecting stones from a field that was circumscribed by thick rope, according to regulations. Perhaps she had made a mistake and come rather too close to the rope as she was bending to pick up the stones. Out of the blue the soldier shot at her, just like that. She fell on her back, her hands pressed to her body, her eyes wide open with fear. 'An attempted escape,' the soldiers said.

'You liars.' There was a murmuring among us.

'Stay where you are, or else it will be your turn!'

We pressed slowly forwards, like a wall. It was too late. Galina was dead, twenty-five years old.

Was the soldier suffering from a hangover, or did he just want to try out his rifle? How unimportant that became once she was dead. The lorry which took us back into the camp in the evening still showed traces of blood. It had taken Galina to the mortuary.

This happened during the Stalin regime when we wore numbers on the back of our clothing. At that time I was 0-392. A printed number on a scrap of material, neatly sewn on the back of my jacket and my black dress. It made it easier to identify us when one of us offended against the camp regulations. This piece of material was about 25 x 12cm in size. Galina no longer needed to wear her number on her back. She was given a label of birch wood, a little docket with her name and the paragraph, 58/1, on it. They tied it all on to her big toe, as they did for all dead persons. Perhaps this was better for her; she had suffered so much during the last weeks.

As was the case every year, the older children had had to leave the children's house. They were to be sent south, to Asiatic Russia, and accommodated there in orphanages. They could not be allowed to grow up with their imprisoned mothers; as free citizens of the Soviet state they had the right to a collective education in a state orphanage.

While the lorry which would transport the children stood in front of the camp gate, we were driven into the huts and locked in. The mothers were allowed to kiss and to embrace their children for the last time. Some, like Galina, had given birth in captivity. Sophia Michailovna brought her son Sasha into the world in a Leningrad prison cell where Sasha's father too had been born. She had still been able to decipher the writing on the cell wall. Other women's children were in arms or just toddling, when they were arrested. Most of the children, however, were fathered by prisoners. But all were mothers watching the transport arrangements, mothers whose children were being taken far into Russia to an orphanage whose address they would not learn until they were released. I cannot forget those ear-splitting cries, sobbing. It was like a mass burial.

Most of these imprisoned mothers had been condemned to ten years in a labour camp, some to only five but many to twenty-five years. Twenty-five years! For most of these mothers this separation would be for ever. How could a young man or a young woman begin to relate to a mother who had been prematurely aged by the years of imprisonment and whom he or she could no longer remember?

8

Festivals had to be celebrated, especially in captivity. All festivals, but Christmas in a very special way. We even celebrated it twice over: our own Christmas festival was celebrated in December; that of the Orthodox Church in January. Every year – apart from 1945 during the train transport – we made the same preparations as we would have done at home. Each day from the beginning of November we dried a slice of our black, moist bread on the stove. This was a real effort for each of us, hungry as we were. Sometimes we could only refrain from eating the slice of bread every other day, but we had to do it, if we were to have our Christmas cake. Naturally we had to avoid being caught with our dried bread by the supervisors who would have suspected us of preparing to escape and put us in prison again. So we were very careful. They did not want prisoners to celebrate festivals. But we always succeeded in drying enough bread to enable us to have our bread cake at Christmas. The recipe was simple.

After work on 24 December, the bread, which was as hard as rock, was broken up with stones or a hammer. This was done as quietly as possible, which was not easy. The pieces were collected in a sack or a pillowcase, and an empty glass was rolled over them until the black, sour bread had been transformed into a fine, flour-like mass. Hot sugar water was poured onto these crumbs – we had saved up our last sugar ration for this purpose – and the cake was already almost finished. The cake mixture obtained in this way was divided into equal portions, during the first years in 'Oskar Meyer' tins and then later in aluminium dishes, and placed in the snow in front of the hut so that it would go cold. With a temperature of -40°C or more, this happened very quickly. The 'cakes' were placed on boards, and Agnes, the most artistically gifted among us, then had the task of decorating them, economically and yet beautifully, with a kind of buttercream. In our little family we also had one or two sick persons who received invalids' rations, which included a daily pat of butter the size of a postage stamp and almost as thin.

Next the Christmas tree was fetched from its hiding place. We had smuggled it into the camp some time before Christmas. At the last moment we decided on the place where the celebrations would take place. This was a necessary precaution to prevent the festivities being betrayed before they had even started, for there were informers everywhere. One year we wanted to have our party in the attic of the children's house; it was risky, to be sure, but also so tempting to keep the party to ourselves and to be wholly undisturbed, free from the noise and perpetual shouting in the huts. The children's house, which was in a corner of the camp, was fenced in, its entrance always guarded. With boldness and skill we could slip in quickly while the guards were being changed and make our way into the boiler house. Agnes, Frossya and Masha were responsible for heating the children's room and took turns to stoke up the giant stove with coal from the mines in and around Inta. This big stove which had to be heated night and day – for the benefit of the young, free Soviet citizens – took up almost the entire space. To the right and left of it, between the wall and the stove, there was a small, narrow space where I often washed myself in secret. It had to be in secret because even this was forbidden: I was supposed to wash myself like all the other women with a litre of water or less per person in the entrance to the hut.

On the left behind the stove there was access to the attic holding the water tanks through a trap door (reached using a ladder). We went in this way on that Christmas Eve; up there, within the wooden partition surrounding the tanks, was where we wished to celebrate. First of all the tree and the cakes were taken up. It was not easy, because there was no light in the attic, but what did that matter, we knew the way in the dark. Then we climbed one after another up the ladder and crept through the opening. The last person, Anne-Marie, had to replace the ladder behind the stove so that we could shut the trap door from above ensuring that nobody down below would have any idea that we were having a party up there. We used a thick rope to pull Anne-Marie up. She pushed against the whitewashed wall with her wet felt boots and left big black footmarks on the white wall. These could not be missed! And after all our care! Those of us who were up above started to laugh at the sight and almost let go of the rope; we supposed that no one would notice; and we laughed and laughed.

We were in the best of spirits when the party began. We not only had our bread cakes, but we also had something to drink! Our Christmas tree was on a stool in the middle of the enclosure. It was adorned by one single candle. It was the first candle in six years. Our cakes were placed in front of it, on a plank on the floor. We sat on the heating pipes that ran along the wooden walls of the enclosure. In one corner was our drink: a wooden bucket full of 'braga', a slightly alcoholic drink which can be made from bread, boiling water and sugar. These ingredients are placed in a large container and left to ferment. With luck, the container, usually a wooden bucket, held fast; without that luck, the bucket would burst some time before Christmas, leaving nothing to drink. Throughout this process there was always the risk of discovery: it was strictly forbidden to produce or to consume alcoholic drinks in the camp, however small the alcohol content might be. This time we were lucky: the bucket had held and we enjoyed our braga. The single candle lit up the room and was reflected in our eyes. As on every Christmas Eve, we sang our old Christmas carols. 'Silent Night' always came first, then the others which followed were easier to sing. It was Christmas. How rich we were, in spite of everything! We had cakes and braga! At the beginning of the party we were still quiet and tried to keep our voices down, but the bucket of braga was gradually emptied and our caution disappeared along with the contents of the bucket. We laughed, chattered and sang ever more loudly. How lovely and warm it was up here! We were no longer prisoners, we were simply laughing, chattering, cheerful young women, as women are irrespective of time and place.

'Hush! I can hear footsteps,' said Masha, interrupting our chatter.

'Surely not, those are not footsteps. Nobody can find us up here!'

'Then who is that talking outside?'

'It can't be. No one can find us here.'

In our fear we all started talking at once. I put out the candle and we waited. Somebody really was coming. We could all hear the steps approaching. We were prepared for the furious voice of an overseer when the trap door was opened. Standing before us was our Lithuanian friend who had only come to wish us a happy Christmas. She had seen the footmarks on the white wall! There was still some braga in the wooden bucket and a place on the heating pipes so the party continued.

'Give me the money! Where's the money? What have you been buying with our money?'

Erna kept on screaming for 'her money'. She could not be serious. No! She must be making a bad joke. Or was she serious? Then I saw the greed in her expression and knew that it was no joke.

'What do you really want from me? Money? Go to Sophia Michailovna's room; you will find the money in the drawer of her table. You can take my share as well. I don't want it any more. I've known for a long time that you weren't up to much, but I had no idea that you were such scum as this!'

At that I turned away from her. A friendship that had lasted for years had been destroyed. Money, money. Where was the money?

For years Masha, Erna, Marlene and I had worked together and had shared with one another every piece of bread that we had earned as an extra with my small 'private laundry'. And now this terrible suspicion!

It was quite a simple matter; for the first time for years, prisoners were paid for some work, but not for all tasks. At that time I did the ironing in the children's house, and this work was very well paid: I received double pay, since I did the work of two prisoners. I was working up to eighteen hours a day then. The stokers, Erna, Marlene and Masha, did much heavier work than I did, though for a shorter time, and the three of them only received one single wage between them. We thought that this was unjust and had come to an agreement with Sophia Michailovna that we should put all three wages together and then divide them between the four of us.

Sophia Michailovna had proposed that I should receive the total wage and then divide it later with the others. When the money was distributed – we never knew beforehand exactly when it was going to arrive – I was busy with some work that was against the regulations. Nobody was allowed to know about it except Sophia Michailovna and myself. At the back in the children's house was a little side room where Sophia Michailovna had locked me in so that nobody could take me by surprise while I was doing this work. Here there were heaps of children's sheets, bedding and napkins. This laundry had been examined by an official inspector and had been declared to be unusable. To indicate this, the laundry had been identified by means of cuts with an axe, so that it should not be presented again at the next inventory, for all these items had been replaced by new ones. It was a question now of fraying out the cuts made by the axe and of darning them in such a way that they looked like a normal tear, or else of putting on irregular patches; in brief the axe blows were so cleverly concealed that the same items of laundry were presented for inspection next year, together with some other items that had traces of normal wear. The new items of laundry which in this way were superfluous could be at our disposal for our personal use. The inventory always tallied! And think of all the things that can be made out of napkins and children's sheets! I made a dress out of three children's grass-green napkins that was so good I could have worn it when I was free. However, I finally left it behind in Russia.

If the wrong people had come to know about the matter, we should inevitably have been imprisoned again, for nothing is more strongly punished in Soviet Russia than theft of state property, and what we were doing was certainly theft. Theft of state property, mind you! That was why no one knew where I was on that day nor what I was doing. Sophia, a Jewish woman from Leningrad, was cunning and careful enough to lock me in for the whole day and to keep the key with her. She had only fetched me out for quite a short time so that I could receive the wretched money; I had put the money at once into the drawer of her table and then let myself be locked up again in my side room so that I could finish my work. And Erna was looking for me and 'her' money. She was telling everyone in the camp that I had her money and had presumably already spent it. When I came into the hut in the evening, one could hear over and over again amid all the shouting the word 'money'.

Yet there was scarcely anything to be bought in the small camp shop; at times there was unappetising red jam made of paste, perhaps tooth powder as well, which we used as face powder. Once there was even cheese, and another time shoes: twenty pairs for 2,000 women. Outside the camp, margarine or bacon could occasionally be bought from ex-prisoners. But really that was all.

This was the cause of the anger and quarrelling, the cursing and the floods of tears.

Some months later she was released from the camp. She departed as if we had never known one another, as a stranger.

Later, in Germany, we met again and talked together once more. For a short time I forgot that only money had any meaning for her.

Anne-Marie. Delicate, red-haired Anne-Marie was standing by the entrance of the fourth camp when we arrived there. She looked pale and very sad. She scarcely showed any emotion at our unexpected reunion – and yet she had come to Inta in the same truck as me.

'How long have you been here in number four?'

'For two years now. It used to be a men's camp.'

'You look so sad, Anne-Marie. What's wrong?'

'Oh, don't ask me. There are many reasons for my sadness.'

'Where are you working?'

'I do general work.'

'All the time?'

'No. I worked in the side bay as an auxiliary nurse for a long time, when this place here was still a camp for men.'

'That was a good job, wasn't it?'

'Of course. It is always a good thing if you can work in the warm. But you have to pay for the privilege'.

A few weeks later Anne-Marie gave birth to two baby girls. One of the twins was stillborn. Genia, the younger one, however, was extremely lively. The dead baby girl was laid in a cardboard box which Marlene buried in secret outside the camp. She took the cardboard box under her arm like a violin case, while she had a spade stuck under her other arm. It was funny and sad.

Anne-Marie was happy to have her little Genia. This delicate little girl was to a certain extent the child of us all; she caused us a great deal of worry at the start of her life, and then later, on the day of the big transport, we all suffered almost as much as Anne-Marie herself. Genia was two and a half. When Anne-Marie saw her again, she was seven years old.

9

'The hay harvest' – I only needed to hear these words to get goose flesh up my back. I shall never forget the millions of tiny flies, nor the acrid smoke of a fire that has been fed with damp wood or wet grass in an attempt to drive away insects. Nor shall I forget that wretched, humid, sultry heat which almost choked us.

It was in July 1954. The time of the midnight sun. The brigades were being assembled for the hay harvest.

One evening after another the Naryadshitza appeared with her list in the huts. Then one particular evening it happened: she read out my name as well. There was no question at all, as far as I was concerned, of exposing myself again to these tortures. Valentina Simeonovna had given me many tips and 'recipes' so that one could become ill when one thought it right to do so. I thought it right now.

All I needed to do was to drink a strong infusion of machorka on the evening before we were due to set out, and the next morning I should not be able to stand up: it would be impossible to send me off to the hay harvest in that condition. I wandered through the camp and came across Gertrud, that sober, practical East Prussian. She was no longer particularly young, being in her forties. Her health was very precarious.

'Are you coming along to the hay harvest too?' she asked me.

'Yes and no,' was my reply.

'Now what's that supposed to mean? Can't you express yourself more clearly?'

'Quite simply, it's like this: yes, because my name was called out yesterday; no, because I haven't the slightest intention of taking part in the hay harvest.'

'What's your plan?'

'On the evening before the group sets off, I shall drink an infusion of machorka with the result that I shan't be able to travel. If you like, I'll make one for you too. All we need to know is the exact day of departure.'

How wrong I was! Gertrud did not want to stay behind at all. Quite the opposite. It seemed to me as if she were almost looking forward to this wretched hay harvest. I considered whether this was through pure ignorance of what awaited her there; she had not come to Inta until 1949 or 1950, much later than me. The years immediately after the war were the worst years in the camp, and it was then that I had been obliged to go to the hay harvest. But the flies and midges of the tundra never change!

Then she told me that she had, in fact, been allocated to a number of hay harvests. She knew as well as I did all the unpleasant features of this work in the tundra. And yet she was determined to join in once again. It seemed that I was the one who was wrong: the work was no longer taking place close to the camp, but much further to the south west. She had the happiest memories of these hay harvests, and unlike me had been to more than one.

'Come on. Come along with me. They give us nets to protect us from the midges. We shall be able to arrange things so that we can stay together. You'll see how fine a hay harvest can be. We have a much better time there than we do here; we are freer.'

Her last words sufficed.

'Agreed!'

I was by no means as keen as she was, but as we were the only two Germans assigned to the hay harvest, I felt almost obliged to go with her, the older and weaker one. I was not led just by the prospect of a little freedom!

It did not take us long to pack. Our 'luggage' consisted of a small bag which was easy to carry around. Ivan's case stayed behind in the camp store room. It was only once a year, mostly in June, that we had our suitcases from the quarters where they were stored. For three or four days then brightly coloured women's clothes fluttered in the wind throughout the camp. But the grey, black camp was full of bright dabs of colour only for a few days. Once they had been given an airing the things were replaced neatly and tidily in the suitcases, and these in their turn were brought back to the store room – until the next year.

It had been like this since 1949; up until then we had been allowed to wear our own clothes – if we had any. But after that the black dress ruled in the women's camp. This black dress already looked a stripy grey and white after just one wash. In time it became almost white, dirty white. The year after, it started again from the beginning: one dress per year, one slip a year, one pair of knickers a year; a pair of felt boots or a wadded jacket every three or four years. For the hay harvest they distributed gum boots – full of holes.

On the day of our departure we assembled as always by the camp gate. We formed two brigades, each of 28 women. Five guards were to accompany us. We were leaving the camp for the duration of summer, that is, for six or seven weeks.

We were searched and counted – that was part of the process, and was taken for granted; the jacket was unbuttoned and we had to let ourselves be searched from head to foot by a woman inspector. Between the breasts, between the legs. It was not quite four o'clock in the morning, two hours earlier than usual. The sky seemed lined with gold; it was one of those wonderful, bright, northern summer nights in which the sun is radiant without causing too much heat. A few lorries were standing ready for us outside the camp. We drove in the direction of Inta.

Two or three hours later we arrived at a river bank.

'The Usa,' somebody said.

Suddenly the road in front of us ceased to exist. Before us an opaque green wall: bushes, trees, impenetrable thicket. To our left was a steep slope, down below the Usa, and leading to it a slippery path. A boat was waiting there. We were hungry and perspiring in our jackets. The gruel we received after getting up never kept us going for long, and the bread ration had been no bigger than usual.

'The boat is much too small to take us all!'

'No, no. We had the same one last year.'

Naturally there was only room for some of us in the boat: for the weakest, for our bags and for three of our five guards.

'The rest are to go on foot,' we were told.

'Where are we supposed to go? There's no road here, not even a path!'

'That doesn't matter. You go straight on, towards the Pechora. There's a landing stage a few kilometres this side of Ust. You'll find a ferry boat waiting for you there. Get on now, hurry up!' one of the soldiers shouted from the boat down below.

There were about thirty women still in the camp, and we tried to make our way through the thicket. If only the bank of the Usa had been less steep, we should have been able simply to wade through the water for a few kilometres, but it was much too steep and consequently out of the question. One of our guards had an axe. He went ahead and hacked a way for us through the undergrowth. The other guard, quite a young man, followed us slowly with his guitar over his shoulder. We lost him on the way. He did not find us again until the next day, God knows how.

The sun burned hotter and hotter. Flies and midges attacked us in swarms. There it was again, this hunger. The hot moist earth steamed, and the kilometres became ever longer.

Gertrud at least was lucky; she was in the boat and what was more still had our bread ration with her. We intended to eat it together on our arrival. When? Where?

It would all be easier if one could foresee the end of this trek. But I could see nothing but bushes and trees: primeval forest. The insects literally consumed us. For them our march was a sheer banquet! My eyes swelled noticeably, and in spite of the long trousers my legs were covered with bites; my fingers looked like thick sausages. If only I had drunk my machorka infusion! Three days of fever and vomiting – but not this torture. Towards three o'clock in the afternoon our young guitarist cracked up. For this reason we too were allowed to have a rest. For thirty minutes. But as soon as you stop moving, the insects became completely mad. And again, as earlier in 1947, we made a densely smoking fire with wet grass and damp wood, in order to drive them away with the smoke.

How much further did we have to go along here?

The older guard did not know either, he just shrugged his shoulders. He was suffering from the insects just as much as we were. His uniform was scarcely any protection; in fact it was even hotter for him than for us. The time was probably getting on for seven o'clock in the evening. We dragged ourselves on ever further – 'straight on, straight on,' as we were told.

Where can the Pechora be? It is big enough, we cannot miss it. But where is it? We went on and on, until we suddenly noticed that we had arrived back at the place where we had halted. We tried to go straight ahead from that point again. The sun was still shining, yellowish now and less burning. It was night time. 'This way, this way!'

Our guard shouted like one demented; he was standing at the small landing stage near the boat.

The view that offered itself to us was breathtaking; in the yellowish-golden light of the midnight sun, the Usa flowing into the Pechora, that mighty primeval river.

We ran down the slope to the boat where the boatman swore at us because we were so late. Nobody took any notice of this; we pushed our way, jostling and shoving, on to the ferry. We all got on. Nobody wanted to be left behind so near to our goal; nobody wanted to miss the moment of arrival, that is, of the selection of sleeping quarters.

I stood at the rear of the ferry. The engine started and the jolt caused me to sway this way and that; however, I regained my balance and looked around at the wide expanse of the landscape about us. I no longer heard the women's chatter, so entranced was I by the beauty of this mighty river whose slight ripples reflected the light of the midnight sun. This yellow-golden light, covering the violet-brown swamps to the right, this light that spread over the giant black pines on the left like a yellow-golden veil. What infinite peace!

I felt and comprehended the infinite quality of this northern landscape. I saw the beauty of the sky and the water, and was happy and thankful, in spite of the years that lay behind me, that I could still be receptive to this beauty. I was alive and still had feeling! I could have been dead or completely apathetic. I made another attempt at 'Our Father' and I could say the prayer almost to the end. I realized that it was a grace. How small and insignificant I seemed to myself. Who indeed was I? Today I was here, tomorrow someone else would be at this spot. How unimportant! All that was important was to see this beauty and to accept the grace with gratitude.

At last we came to the end of our boat-crossing. The bank was steep and full of undergrowth. We scrambled as quickly as possible up the slope. When we arrived at the top, the way went straight down again into a valley, then we crossed a stream, and again we went uphill. The hilly landscape with its gentle rippling, resembled the Pechora itself.

But the flies and midges did not forget us!

Would we ever arrive? One more hill and then, a bit further down, the stable. Adjoining it a small cottage. We were greeted by shouts of joy. Our comrades had been there quite a time. Gertrud, bless her, had kept a place for me up in the hayloft, just near the entrance, so that we had air and light. I climbed up the ladder and looked out: just opposite were horses in an enclosure. There were eight or nine, together with a foal. To the left, the tundra and a few old trees. Further to the left the Pechora was gleaming; to the right a gentle slope.

'Further down there is a pool where you can wash,' Gertrud said and pointed down the slope.

That was something that did not have to be repeated to me. I bounded down the ladder, three rungs at a time. On reaching the edge of the pool, I took off my dress, my long trousers and shoes. I only intended to wash myself really, but the water's edge was deceptive: I had scarcely put my foot into the water when I went down in a hole. I was wet right up to my hair and started to swim in this comforting water. I had forgotten how pleasant swimming is. The insect bites no longer stung! I had the feeling of being free. Free! I was swimming! At last I could pray.

Gertrud was right. A few hours later we were not woken as usual by the noise of two iron bars being knocked together, but by a human voice. How comforting! Like a flash I was down the ladder, so that I could plunge straight into my pool, before doing anything else.

The other brigade spent the night beneath us in the stable. After the morning soup insect nets were distributed. At last. I looked across at the horses: Maxim, the foal, was rubbing against his mother Toska, a big, broad working mare. Each brigade was assigned four horses; we had Maxim and Toska. Four volunteers from each brigade were responsible for the horses with which they were working. They had to be curried, led to work and harnessed, all things which were completely new to me. Ukrainians certainly know how to deal with horses, and as there were many Ukrainians in each of the two brigades, the question of personnel for the horses was soon decided.

'You should have volunteered to look after a horse,' Gertrud said, 'that is the easiest work!'

'But I don't know anything about horses!'

'So what? I would have shown you!'

There was no doubt that she could manage horses well, only she felt that she was too old and weak to do so.

'A pity! It's too late now!'

We went towards the tundra. After a few kilometres tufts of grass sprang up here and there before us. The brigade leaders marked out on the ground a rectangle of about seven metres by four metres.

Spades were distributed which had been brought along behind us in a clattering ox-drawn cart. I could see neither scythes nor rakes. What was happening here? We had to dig out a hole following the measurement of the rectangle that had been staked out.

'What's that for?' I asked Gertrud.

'For the grass of course. You'll see tomorrow.'

We dug and dug. For hours. I had enough of it. I could carry on no longer. But the hole had to be finished before we could be taken back to our 'stable'. A light wind drove away the wretched flies. I would never have believed that the hole could have been ready by evening and if it were, then it would definitely not be thanks to my efforts: I had long been unable to carry on and had given up. I once more regretted that I had not drunk my machorka infusion. The Ukrainian women were in any case stronger than I was; let them finish this job on their own. I had to preserve my strength if I wanted to last out until the end of my sentence. I already had behind me nine years of hard labour. During that time I had been too often reminded that prisoners who held on for years collapsed and died shortly before or just after their release. I wanted to live, and what's more to live on as a free woman.

The next morning the real hay harvest began. Four girls on horseback formed the vanguard, with the supervisor also on horseback at their head. They and the horses soon disappeared in the hilly tundra. The ox cart, laden this time with scythes and rakes, followed slowly. Near the hole rakes and scythes were distributed by the brigade leaders. Gertrud was given a scythe as she knew how to handle it. I accepted a rake; that was an implement I could still use!

We worked together. The task now was to find and to mow tufts of grass in the tundra which consisted largely of moss and bog. Gertrud mowed, and I raked the grass together in little heaps. While we were busy at this work, other women were constructing crude sledges which were then fastened on to the horses; on each side of the horse a long branch was affixed whose twigs and leaves dragged along the ground and were intertwined with other branches to make a 'sledge'. The grass was loaded on to this and dragged along to the hole.

I very quickly understood that Gertrud was right: I should have offered to take charge of a horse. This was by far the easiest work. One woman grasped the horse by the halter, holding in her other hand an axe which she used to clear a path through the bushes and undergrowth to the hole. Another woman went behind the sledge and she loaded the heaps of grass onto it, taking care that not too much fell off before they reached the hole into which the grass was thrown as if into a silo.

The ox had as fine a time as could be imagined. When the hole was about a quarter filled with grass, he was allowed go down and to eat as much as he wished; the main thing was that he should trample on the grass which was then covered with willow branches.

'And what is that for?' I turned to Gertrud who should know.

'For fermentation!'

Eventually evening came, and we returned to our stable, tired and hungry. But there was my pool. It was the same every evening. As soon as I was in the water, I no longer felt the countless insect bites, nothing but the happiness of being alive. Each time I was surprised and thankful that I was still capable of feeling this. After nine years in a labour camp one became a sort of robot, but I was alive again.

On the third day the girl who was in charge of Toska, the mare, for the outside work broke a leg. She was transported to the nearest village by ox cart. She had to be replaced.

'You go and volunteer! You can lead Toska and I will go behind with the rake!'

I volunteered, and Toska was allocated to me. It was all right leading the horse with one hand and brandishing the axe with the other. But then in the evening, when everyone mounted their horses, and I had never been on horseback before, then I really was afraid! Toska had neither saddle nor stirrup – only a halter.

'You mount from the left, always a little to the rear. When you are up, hold tight to the horse's neck, as far forward as you can. I'll help you to get up.'

And that was the end of my riding lesson. Gertrud held her hands folded together so that I could place my foot on them and from there swing myself on to the broad-backed Toska.

'Nobody must notice that this is your first time on a horse, otherwise it will all be over tomorrow, and for two months long we shall have to do the heavy work!'

'Yes, yes, I know. I'll do what I can.'

The good Toska trotted along slowly and at an even pace; Maxim stayed by her side. In front of me were two Ukrainian women on their horses. It was not their first time on horseback! Behind me was the third Ukrainian who no doubt had noticed something of my uncertainty. Suddenly she struck Toska's broad backside with a willow cane; Toska at once started galloping.

'Always keep well forward, close to the neck.' I repeated my riding instruction and slid forward as far as I could on the galloping horse. Then I saw the thick branch across the narrow track, just at the level of my head. Toska was still galloping. There were only two possibilities: either I let myself fall backwards on to Toska's broad rear, or I would knock my head against the branch. I instinctively decided for the first possibility and let myself go backwards while my legs clung round Toska's neck like a pair of tongs. I was terrified, but I did not fall off!

Two weeks later there was nothing more to be mown in this area. We had to leave our stable, and I had to leave my pool too. We were loaded into a huge barge and travelled along the Pechora. We lay down in the ship's hold: on one side the prisoners, on the other the horses. But they were not the same horses. Toska and Maxim (who had filched my white-cheese sandwich, the first since my imprisonment) remained behind in their enclosure opposite the stable. It was becoming cooler, and the nights longer. In the hold down below there was black night. It began to rain. The ship's deck let the rain through. Soon we were soaked through. I was reminded of the darkness and cold in the truck on the rail journey.

Gertrud and I had managed to lie close together again. On our side of the hold it was only possible to crawl. A wooden partition had been put up at the front part of the hold, where it was higher. Through the chinks of the wood candlelight was shining. I could see a table, empty bottles lying around cigarette ends, ash everywhere, and a soldier's camp in the midst of it all. One of our guards was snoring loudly. He lay sprawling on a bench, evidently dead drunk. Two others were shouting at each other. Our young guitarist was singing in a tearful voice one of those melancholy Russian songs. The sleeping soldier suddenly woke up and fell upon the young soldier with a loud curse. The table fell over, bottles were broken, the candles went out, but the brawling continued.

With a feeling of revulsion I crawled to the middle of the hold and went on deck for a breath of air. A tug pulled our barge. The night was grey and dark. It was drizzling. We moved forwards only very slowly. But after a short time it stopped raining. The moon appeared between wisps of cloud.

I stayed on deck a long time, quite alone. The river banks were completely deserted. No lights, no houses.

The next morning we put ashore. The bank rose steeply, and we had difficulty in dragging up the horses. This time I was allocated a light-brown mare with a long yellow tail, Gonka, who was much younger and thinner than Toska. After the horses had been tethered on top of the bank we went back to the barge to be given bread and soup.

In this terrain holes were no longer dug out. We were further south, which meant the grass could be dried on wooden poles. There were many types of deciduous trees as well as the familiar pines and birches. The mowing too was much easier, since there were already established, if small, meadows. No longer did we have to struggle to discover each tuft of grass.

Gertrud and I loaded up our sledge in the same way as before and went with it to the wooden poles where two other women were hanging up the grass. In the evening we returned to our barge. We had been forbidden to swim because of the Pechora's strong current. But what did I care: the water of the Pechora was much colder than the water of my little pool. On one occasion I was carried away by the current. Faster and faster. I needed all my strength to regain the bank.

A soldier happened to be walking past where I had left my things. He beckoned to me with his rifle to come to the shore. From a distance I tried to make it clear to him that I did not intend to come out of the water naked as long as he was still there. At last he understood, turned round and went! Later on he told me that he had believed at first that a deer was drifting in the water.

'I almost shot it,' he said.

Already our soldiers would sit around a fire warming their hands. But I was still swimming in the Pechora every day until the first snow. What delight!

The sun was setting earlier every evening, the nights becoming longer, the same scenes being repeated: the wooden enclosure with the candlelight, the drunk and brawling soldiers. I would go on deck to be alone. Almost without a sound the barge moved through the still calm water. For the first time I thought about the future. For years we had been sustained only on the past.

'I have one more year. Where will they send me? To Siberia, like Valentina Simeonovna? Shall I be left in Inta, like Marlene? To Germany?'

I must not think about it, I had to remain rational, otherwise I should not survive. Strange, my mother had still not written to me. Parcels had come, but not a single line. And then images came to my mind again: the truck, Sangorodok, Vanya, Valentina who dared not write to me any more, and all the dead. I saw the nocturnal Pechora, the sky hung with clouds, and the calm of this infinity came over me as well.

Suddenly I felt cold. I went back to the hold and lay down close to Gertrud who was fast asleep, in order to warm myself against her.

We lived this life for three weeks: in the daytime work, midges, smoking fires, gruel and the eternal moist black bread. Each day I rode long distances through the tundra with my mare Gonka – so young, so sensible, so full of life. I used to say to Gertrud: 'If someone asks for me, just tell them that I've gone in search of grass!'

The tundra is so wide and so endless that nobody noticed our absence, neither the brigade leader nor our supervisor, and yet Gonka and I stayed away longer each day. While I rode through the tundra, Gertrud slept under a tree or else out in the mild late summer sunshine. But the really festive time did not start until the evening, when Gonka and I bathed in the Pechora. What a good listener she was when I talked to her! I was alive and I loved this life. How glad I was that I had not drunk the machorka infusion.

One morning after I had spent part of the night on deck, as I so often did, I suddenly saw houses appear on the left back of the river.

The barge was moving forwards, but only slowly. To judge from the smoke that was rising from the chimneys of these mud huts, breakfast soup was being prepared everywhere. At the landing stage a little girl of about five was standing and watching the horse's manoeuvring; she had the expressionless, apathetic face of an old woman. Her child's eyes reflected the suffering of humanity it seemed to me.

The soldiers, drunk as they nearly always were, ordered us to leave the boat. It was not until later that the horses were taken ashore on the opposite bank. We went through the sad village where there were neither gardens nor flowers, and reached our quarters.

There was nobody to be seen in the street. A dead village? I felt the glances of the anxious people who behind their small windows were trying curiously to discover a familiar face among the prisoners passing by. In this village ex-prisoners had been compulsorily settled. These former prisoners were afraid to lose their liberty by talking to us. It was a completely remote village where a boat might pull in during the summer once a fortnight; in the winter they were completely cut off from the world. They stayed in their huts and drank vodka, as long as there was any.

We came to a halt before a slightly larger house. A village hall? Perhaps. We arranged our sleeping quarters on the floor of the largest room: arranged in layers, as in the truck. Our supervisors slept in the adjoining room and had to make their way over our feet to get to their rooms when they came back at night drunk. Behind the house there was a shed, the public latrine and behind that a track led into the village. There I met Irmgard, the 'country egg' as she had been mockingly nicknamed. She was a tall, strongly built, East Prussian, country woman. Very helpful, always friendly, she was pleased to see me, but immediately looked around to make sure that nobody was watching. She had been given a five-year sentence, and had married after being set free becoming the mother of a baby boy. She had lived with her husband, a Pole, in this remote, forgotten village for the past two years. Again she glanced fearfully to right and left.

'No,' I said, 'nobody can see us here. You needn't be afraid. I won't delay you any longer. Goodbye!'

I left her; she should not risk her pseudo-liberty on my account.

Was this to be my lot next year, after my liberation? For this was the freedom granted to someone who had completed their period of detention. After seven years' imprisonment Marlene had been set free in 1952. She was not allowed to leave Inta until 1955. For three years she was only allowed to move within a radius of forty kilometres and had to report once a week at the commandant's office.

But most of the released prisoners were sent to remote villages, like this sad, muddy village here with its twenty houses at most. No, not that, surely! Even the camp was preferable to that; there at least I had human contacts, and, having nothing to lose, could retain my inner freedom.

The women and girls were still mowing grass while I continued my escapades with Gonka, my young mare. A mood of sadness overcame me at the thought that we should soon be brought back to the camp. Gertrud, on the other hand, was looking forward to this; she who had persuaded me to come along to the hay harvest could scarcely wait to be in the camp again. She was too old and ill to be sleeping in the holds of barges or on bare floors. Ailing as she now was, she looked upon the camp as a refuge, with its huts and plank beds, covered with sacks which we had filled with shavings. But how happy I should be, for this wonderful summer to last a few more weeks! What did the flies and the swollen eyes matter to me? Or the drunken soldiers? What did any of that matter compared with the strong, new, pulsating life which I had experienced by the Pechora.

10

After the death of Stalin in 1953 we were allowed to remove the number tabs sewn on to the back of our clothes. We were called by our names again. A short time afterwards millions of political prisoners were released: it was the first amnesty of this kind since the Soviet Union had come into existence.

First those who had been given five-year sentences were released, then those who had been condemned to ten years and had already served seven of them. Those condemned to fifteen or twenty-five years breathed again and could now in turn count on a remission of their sentence.

Week after week great columns of prisoners made their way to liberty through the camp gate; they could either stay in Inta or else they were sent to Siberia. Those who had only been given short sentences were allowed to return to the place where they had been arrested.

All this resulted in far-reaching changes.

At that time I had already served two-thirds of my sentence, and I counted on my immediate release. Each week I waited for my name to be read out. The camp was already nearly empty. Where once two thousand women had lived, now only about a hundred remained.

As in every prison in the world, incredible and often contradictory rumours were current. This is simply a part of prison life, like the plank bed and the bucket. The most beautiful, but unfortunately also the least credible of all these rumours was this: in one of the men's camps somebody had said that the German prisoners were being collected up and sent back to Germany. If that were true! No, it would be better not to think too much about it, the disappointment would be almost unbearable!

Why would they not allow me to live as a free person in Inta or send me to Siberia, for that matter? If only I could walk down a street on my own, without a guard with a rifle over his shoulder. After all I had long since served the two-thirds of my sentence necessary for an early release, just like the others who had already left the camp. They had not made any distinction between us as far as work was concerned. I had had to buckle down to it just like the Russian women. In that respect we were all the same. Why was this distinction being made all of a sudden between me and the Russians? I was the only German woman in my camp who could have a claim to be released and they were not releasing me.

Soon there were only about thirty women left. Only Germans – and Agnes, the German who had been born in Russia. None of us were given work any more. We sat around in the hut, had no contact any longer with the outside world, and consequently were without news or rumours. Nothing is worse than to be waiting without occupation for something indefinite. Much better to be out working. We had been going on like this for a month, the tension in the hut becoming increasingly unbearable, until: 'Wait, I've got an idea,' I cried out suddenly.

'What sort of an idea?' I was asked.

'Just wait, you'll soon find out.'

I went, indeed I ran, straight to the camp officer and asked for a personal interview. He was sitting behind his desk, while to his right, on a bench by the wall, a non-commissioned officer was dozing.

'What do you want?' he asked me.

'You know, my question is a very awkward one. People are saying here everywhere, that is, I have heard it said, but don't know whether it is true, well, I have heard that we are to be sent to Germany and I should like to know what I must do to stay here.'

His dumbfounded expression was wonderful to see! He must have thought I had gone out of my mind. He got up, looking at me in complete bewilderment. Even the dozing non-commissioned officer had stood up in order to peer at me. They could hardly believe the evidence of their own eyes.

'Well, why do you want to stay here then?'

'Quite simply because I feel at home here now. I have friends here, I know the language, why should I not go on living here? I don't know post-war Germany. I am afraid I may not make contacts, but here I know that I can live.'

'Good, I understand. If you want to stay here, you must at once write a petition to Moscow (and he gave me the address!) and make a request for Russian citizenship. Perhaps you will then be left here.

But hurry up!'

'Thank you very much,' and I disappeared at a smart pace.

I raced back to the hut. The loveliest of all rumours was true after all: 'We're going to Germany, I've had it directly from the camp boss,' I shouted into the noise around me.

His reply had been unequivocal and clear, but Moscow would have to wait a long time for my petition.

In November 1954, only a few days after I had put my question to the camp boss, we left the camp in the evening. Large wet snowflakes fell on our faces and enveloped us. Agnes remained behind alone. She stood at the gate, and we both wept.

The train was ready and waiting not far from the camp on the railway tracks that we had laid; a goods train as before, ten years ago. It went slowly past Inta. Inta, where I myself had worked on almost every house, on almost every street. Inta, a town which had not even been a village when we arrived, disappeared behind me in the night. Homesickness? Nostalgia? Already? Impossible!

'Strange, we seem to be going north, not south.'

It seemed impossible to us. We were unwilling to believe it, and yet the train was travelling northward – so not towards Germany, after all?

But the officer, as he was standing beside me when I was just going to climb into the truck, had said to me in a quiet voice: 'Take some snow with you. There isn't any where you are going.'

The truck, as usual a cattle truck, stank wretchedly. We had of course no light, but the lights of the town of Inta, which were slowly getting smaller and smaller, showed clearly that we were really travelling ever further north.

The next morning we reached Abes. We were taken to a small camp, which was not far from the railway line. It had formerly been a camp for sick and elderly women who were no longer able to perform heavy work. Transports came in daily from Vorkuta and other camps in the area. Germans, only Germans. Perhaps Abes was only a collecting centre. We began to hope again. Surely we should get to Germany.

Weeks passed. We were sent out to work again. I was pleased, since only in this way could the period of never-ending waiting be tolerated.

Christiane and I were assigned to the serving of food; later we worked in the Kipyatilka, where water was boiled and distributed. These were all small, light tasks, which we did gladly. Occasionally I had to go out and clear snow from the railway track. My glance travelled along these lines which went so straight and so infinitely far to the south-west. Behind me, to the north-east, I could see the Komis, the inhabitants of this district, who from a distance looked like Eskimos, in their clothes of reindeer skins and with their sledges drawn by reindeer or dogs.

Incredible how powerfully these railway lines acted upon me. Again I strained to look towards the south-west, to where I thought Europe lay. Europe? Germany? Would we ever see them again? It seemed almost impossible. We had seen too much. And again I was beset by doubts. One evening, when I came back to the hut from my railway lines, a little black cat was lying on my place. I did not want her and chased her off. Two minutes later she was there again, a little black bow-legged cat with amber-coloured eyes. Again I chased her away from my place, but then I gave up; she stayed and at night draped herself around my neck like a warm shawl.

And once again rumours were rife. All Germans were being sent to Central Asia, Karaganda. There was a damp, humid heat there the whole year through, it was said, and only a few of the prisoners who had lived for years in the north could tolerate it. Not a day passed without one of them dying, especially women over forty.

Suddenly another rumour arose: that all the sick and infirm Soviet Prussian prisoners who were here in Abes would be sent to Karaganda, even before the Germans. At that Christiane and I determined to prevent our Lithuanian friend Stassya, who had a bad heart, from leaving Abes. She would not have survived Karaganda.

The most difficult problem was finding out the exact time when the transport would leave. For Stassya would have to become ill at the earliest on the evening before or at the latest on the morning of the departure. Our self-induced illnesses never lasted longer than two or three days. Of course, one could also have hacked off a foot or a hand. That had often happened in the early days, but one did not gain much benefit from that: a new trial, an even more severe punishment.

The offence: sabotage.

It simply could not be determined whether and when this transport was setting off for Karaganda. As so often, we lived in complete uncertainty. Everything was ready, the syringe, milk, and we had also worked out the hiding place where we would give Stassya the injection, for it would not do for anyone to surprise us in the act.

'The transport is definitely tomorrow!'

'How can you be so sure? Who told you, Christiane?'

'Nobody. But they've already started distributing suitcases to the next hut. Somebody will soon appear here as well and make an announcement. All the Russian women are being summoned. So it's quite clear that tomorrow is the day. I'll fetch the milk. We've got to hurry now.'

The three of us went into the room where water was heated. I was on night duty, and nobody would go there then. Christiane gave Stassya the injection of milk in the upper part of her left thigh. That same night our 'patient' had a temperature of over 40°C. The camp doctor diagnosed a form of influenza, of a type hitherto unknown in those northern parts. He had not seen the huge red spot on Stassya's thigh. As big as a peaked cap. Poor Stassya, she suffered terribly. Her temperature kept rising; we wiped the sweat off her brow. But now we were really frightened and, worst of all, the train for the transport did not come.

Stassya only recovered very slowly. The next time we would have to think of something else. We made up our minds that we would simply hide her. Neither the water-storage room nor the attic seemed to us to be safe enough. Sometimes women who wanted to avoid transportation hid themselves in snow caverns; in that case only a good friend knew where this cave was and took her food and hot water regularly so that she should not freeze. But we had too little snow on the camp premises, for all the mountainous heaps of snow had just been removed from the site, and a snow cavern would have been discovered at once.

Then we had the idea of simply hiding her in our hut; no one would suspect that she might be under a mattress. That was a completely new hiding place. As I worked at night in the water-storage room, I was allowed to sleep in the day time and did not need to get up for the roll call, either in the morning or in the evening. The camp regulations were less strict now than in the times of Stalin. So we concealed Stassya very early in the morning – around us everybody was still sleeping – underneath my mattress, a sack that was tightly packed with shavings. I placed myself cautiously upon it and went to sleep. Nobody would suspect that Stassya was under my mattress and I myself was entitled to sleep the whole day.

Like all those who had received the summons, Stassya too had been given her case and had then had to bring it to a certain room so that it could be searched. Here the cases stayed until the journey started. She would have liked to have fetched it away from there, but that would have been too risky, so we left it. At last the train came and a search was made for Stassya. In the water-storage room, in the washhouse, in the attic. They came several times into our hut to look under all the beds. Without success. Now and again, I gave the half suffocated Stassya a signal; she put her head out from beneath the mattress and drew a few deep gulps of air.

In the meantime evening had come. It was said in the camp that the train had departed. Without Stassya. A German woman sat down on the plank bed facing me and said: 'Listen, you are friendly with Stassya, you must know where she is. She can come out now; it's all over, in any case.'

'Of course I know where she is, that's obvious. But I am certainly not going to tell you.'

It was known throughout the camp that this woman was an informer. I had hardly replied to her when Stassya, flushed and bathed in perspiration, looked out from beneath the mattress; she had not noticed that the other woman was still there. The German left the hut. Stassya crept back under my mattress. A soldier entered the hut and came directly to my place.

'Stand up at once!' he shouted at me.

'I only get up when an officer tells me to. I am entitled to lie down until it's time for me to start working.'

He came back with an officer. I refused to get up. The two of them dragged me from my mattress. Stassya was taken off by the two men.

Where were they taking her? To the train? To the cells? We were not able to follow her. How should we find out?

The German woman came back. She went down on her knees before me and protested her innocence: 'I swear to you that I have not betrayed you and Stassya', she said, lifting up her right hand.

She sickened me so much that I did not even reply to her. Two soldiers and an officer approached us.

'Goldacker and Senkpiehl, come along!'

How well informed they were that they even knew our surnames! They took us to the cells, and when we were in the narrow corridor Christiane shouted at the top of her voice: 'Stassya, Stassya!'

As we were being pushed into our cell, we could just hear Stassya replying. Thank God she was in the camp. Her suitcase was going to Karaganda without her.

Ten days later it was Christmas, the tenth Christmas in prison.

We were still waiting for our transport. Time stood still. No more rumours, no more transports. Was Abes the terminal station? As usual, we had a small fir tree. This time it was decorated with candles; some of us had received Christmas candles in our Red Cross parcels. We sang the old Christmas carols, ate our bread cake and drank 'braga' – openly. Why should we be afraid? We had nothing more to lose.

Our New Year's wish, for each one of us, was the same as it had always been during the last ten years. 'May the coming year bring you liberty.'

Weeks went by. Nothing stirred. A few women made up their minds not to work any more. They called upon us all to go on strike. Christiane and I were against this. We did not want to lounge about in the huts without working. We still had unpleasant memories of the last long weeks in Inta. We decided to continue with our work in the water-storage house.

Olga, a German woman who had come with the transport from Vorkuta and had been the first to call for a strike, threatened us. We made fun of her and her threats and went on quietly with our work, until the day when a large kitchen knife disappeared – it was found in the snow near the water-storage house. Subsequently we felt cold shivers down our spine.

The days crept slowly by, endlessly long days and nights. February 1955. As each day passed, our hope of being transported back to Germany diminished. It was like being in a stinking pond which had no outflow. Frau R from Austria cheered us up by recounting stories. She could tell stories and recite poems wonderfully.

Then, suddenly and within a single hour, we had to board the train for the transport from Abes. We were leaving our Lithuanian and Latvian friends behind – and my little black bow-legged cat. I would have so liked to take her with me. The train was waiting outside on the track in front of the camp. Christiane and I were lucky; we managed to find places on the boards, close to the window. But the train did not leave.

This wretched counting of heads was unbearable. It was really ridiculous; who would try to stay here, now that we must be going back to Germany? Nobody would have thought of hiding in Abes.

A jolt, and we were off – towards the south. Thank God! We were leaving the north, the tundra. Never again would we experience this infinite expanse which had impressed me so deeply in its enormity. We went on and on. No villages nor towns, only snow and the distant expanse, ancient trees, at first on their own, and then whole forests. How beautiful this northern landscape was. Then came huts, fenced with barbed wire. How much tragedy lay behind all this! The further we travelled southwards, the denser became the vegetation. One evening the train went more slowly. It was not yet completely dark; the village by the railway line reminded me of the deserted village by the Pechora. A man trudged staggering through the deep snow. Was he drunk? At the end of his strength? He fell heavily into the snow and remained lying there. He would be found the next day, or possibly not until the summer – dead, but at liberty.

11

We went ever further south. Should we not soon be turning to the west?

After ten days the train finally stopped in the middle of a forest. I climbed out of the van, holding Ivan Ivanovich's case firmly in my hand. Nothing but snow and thick, impenetrable forest surrounded us. No station! The other vans remained locked up. It was only we women who trudged through the deep snow into the forest. No track, no path. Only snow and trees.

Where were we? Where were we being taken? Was this the end? Perhaps. Everything that we had heard, the return to Germany – after all, these were only rumours; one was never sure in this country. And yet how pleasant it was to be marching like this in the fresh, winter air. I breathed it in hungrily. How much longer? They could quite simply leave us here, shoot us down and bury us in the snow. That was quite simple. But why had we dragged our suitcases along? Whatever for, if this march was to be our last?

Then suddenly huts rose up before us! Real huts, as we had known them and been used to them for years. We were coming to a camp that had been evacuated a short time previously. Still only Germans. Now we were convinced that we were on the way to Germany.

For the first time in ten years each of us had a whole place to herself for sleeping. The next day we were summoned to work. This time we were all of one mind and refused to do a stroke of work for the Soviets.

We were tugged and dragged, one after another, to the great gate; and one after another ran back to our huts, once the guard had released us (he had to go for assistance). For us it was a game, and soon our guards had had enough and left us in the huts.

They sent for inspectors from Moscow. We were all sent into the canteen: two successive sessions were planned so that those who could not be accommodated for the first one would also be able to enjoy the lecture by one of the officers. I came into the canteen with the first group and listened attentively to the officer's remarks.

'It is true there has been an amnesty for political prisoners, but it does not apply to you here. You will all stay here until the end of your sentence and work every year so that you can in this way pay back your debt to the Soviet state. Later, when you have served your fifteen or twenty-five years, we shall decide whether we shall send you back to Germany.'

Soon loud laughter and whistling could be heard from all corners of the room. It was in vain that the officer tried to continue his discourse: 'You will all work and work incessantly, and you won't stop working before you have expiated your guilt. When you have shown yourselves worthy of a pardon, we shall decide about your further fate.'

Mocking laughter, heckling, general chaos. He was never able to finish his lecture.

Laughing and shouting we left the canteen. The second session that had been planned was cancelled; instead we were summoned individually to be interviewed by the four officers from Moscow.

'What story will you tell, if we allow you to go on to Germany?'

'Me?' I asked innocently. 'The whole truth, nothing but the truth!'

There was a pause during which I examined with amusement the facial expressions of the four officers; at first they showed surprise, and then noticeable disquiet. No one said a word. After I had enjoyed to the full this quiet and the effect of my words, I slowly went on: 'The first years were terrible, but I was fortunate enough to survive. Later on I got used to my existence as a prisoner. And today I am happy – you can believe me or not, as you please – to have learned the language of Pushkin and Lermontov.'

I had the impression that the officers facing me were breathing sighs of relief.

A little while after the visit from the Moscow officers we decided that we would work after all. Not indeed out of blind obedience; no, but because the period of waiting passed more quickly in this fashion. We only worked as much as we actually wanted to. It was pleasant to go out of the camp in the morning and trudge through the melting snow to the nursery garden nearby. The snow thawed, and the air almost smelled of spring, a long forgotten smell. So time went by: we went out, did a certain amount of work, and came back to the camp in the evening. How many more days would this waiting last? Where had they taken the men who had come with us from the far north and whose vans stayed locked when we were in the midst of the forest? Our imaginations supplied the answers to these questions; we made bets: 'I'll bet you a real leather handbag,' said Anna, 'that we shall be able to take a stroll together down the Kurfürstendamm in June.'

'I say, not before the middle of August.'

'It's all the same to me; the main thing is, we get back home for Christmas.'

This was at the end of March. In April we finally left this completely isolated camp.

The men were already waiting by the train, which was ready to take us. Of course the endless counting of heads started again. And yet it was not the same. We were almost completely indifferent to it.

The van into which we climbed was no different in any way from those we had experienced previously yet – and I no longer remember which one of us started – suddenly we were all singing. When the song was finished, a soldier knocked on the van outside and asked us to carry on. We sang full of joyful anticipation for Germany and Europe. Then the train moved on towards the west for days and nights until we arrived at Potma.

When I got out of the van and breathed in the fresh spring air, I lost consciousness for a moment. In the camp to which we were taken the women were making bed covers and uniforms. Day and night the prisoners here were compelled to sit and sew behind their sewing machines. We newcomers were allocated work outside the camp, in the fields and forests. In that particular camp I began my personal strike; I did not go out to work for even a single day. I deserved to have some time to myself. It was a long time since I had served the two-thirds of my sentence which were sufficient to justify my release. Other women, Russians, were all already free, but I was not. With what justification were they still holding on to me here? I hid myself during the morning roll call, which was not difficult. The fact that the number of prisoners always tallied may be because they only attached value to exactitude when it was a matter of a departing transport; thus I was left in peace.

Some of those who went out daily to work were given the task of sorting potatoes, a very profitable form of work. Every evening they hid a few potatoes in the pockets of their jackets and brought them into the camp. We were saving them for a potato salad at Whitsun; I received them and guarded them carefully.

On Whit Saturday I went to the kitchen and procured a large saucepan, in order to cook our potatoes in the little 'parcels' kitchen (the Russian prisoners frequently had flour or other cereal products sent to them, and in consequence a small kitchen had been set up within the camp, only for 'parcels'). It was a long time before my eight kilograms of potatoes were properly cooked. At last they were ready, and I entered my hut, bearing the big, steaming saucepan.

Something was wrong here, I noticed at once.

'What's going on here?' I turned to the first person I encountered.

'There's a search on. They are looking for potatoes.'

No, anything but that! What was I to do now? Go back to the 'parcels' kitchen? Too late. That really would draw attention to me.

So I went to my section of the hut which had not yet been searched. I did not have a moment to lose. I put the heavy, steaming saucepan on to my bed, and placed the pillow and myself on top of it. I just had time to tie a towel round my head, then I lowered myself on to pillow and saucepan, and let my gaze go vacant – seriously ill.

I had just settled myself down (extremely uncomfortably) when they arrived. Fortunately they did not start on my side, so the potatoes had time to cool off a bit. I really did feel bad now; if they were looking for potatoes and they found me with such a quantity, that would be seen as theft of state property and would lead to another conviction – and just now, so soon before my release. I was in a cold sweat as they came nearer, looked under my plank bed, opened the drawer of my bedside table, and took my little knife away from me.

'What a cheek! I need that for my potatoes,' I thought. 'Usually they only take what they are looking for at the time, and today it's potatoes they want, not knives.'

Fear made me bold. I said, 'Hold on a minute; leave me my little knife, you surely don't think I could kill anybody with that!'

'Be quiet, for heaven's sake!' my neighbour said, giving me a nudge. She really was ill.

'All right,' the soldier said, putting the knife back and continuing his search with the next bed.

Whew!

In the evening my friends came and asked: 'What about the potatoes?'

'The potato salad is ready,' I said proudly.

During the last weeks in Potma there were frequent inspections of one sort or another during which I kept on asking questions about my release. In the end the camp authorities put me in the cells during inspections. The camp boss himself had already had enough of me. Every day I went to his office and placed myself insolently before him, with both my hands in the trouser pockets of the new tracksuit which I had received from the Red Cross.

How happy this man must have been when one fine morning in June he could push Sonia and me off to another camp. We had to go by train, this time a real passenger train, but unfortunately the journey was a very short one. We were still in the Potma area. We had heard some time earlier that there was another camp not far from ours, said to be only for foreigners. According to our information, this was the last camp; from here transports went regularly to the west, or so it was said.

'Damn it!' I said to Sonia. 'This camp is not an assembly camp at all. It looks just like a prison.'

'Is your conscience clear?'

'Mine? Yes, of course. But with these people you've got to be ready for anything; you never know where you are. What about you, Sonia?'

'My conscience is just as clear, or just as not clear, as yours. If they want to, they will always find something to accuse us of.'

We came to a big wooden door. No barbed wire. Behind it, a two-storey stone house, not a hut. Behind the barred windows could be seen women who were looking down at us inquisitively. There was no doubt about it; this place was a prison.

Sonia let herself be conducted into the cell without resisting. I demanded to talk to an officer. I was not going to let myself be locked up again in a prison without any explanation or warrant. In the normal course of events I should have been at liberty long before this. I would just wait in front of the prison until someone came. Neither the soldier who had accompanied us nor the one who was receiving us knew quite what they should do. Finally one of them started telephoning. A little later he was sent a reinforcement. Now there were three of them against me.

'Oh, do come inside,' Sonia shouted from her cell. 'It isn't all that bad here. The women who are here are all in the same position as us: they've finished their sentences and are waiting for a transport back home. You needn't worry about coming on in. It really isn't as bad as all that.'

'I want to have an explanation from an officer first.'

The soldier who had just come turned to me and said: 'Today is Saturday. The officers have all gone off duty.' That was certainly a lie, but what was I to do against three men?

So there I was in prison again, as I had been when I was arrested ten years previously. In the cell seven women were lying on a few planks that had been pushed close together and placed obliquely. And Sonia had said that it was not so bad here! The key had scarcely turned in the lock before I began to storm furiously: 'I demand to see an officer, an officer.'

In the end they all joined in and shouted, like me, for an officer until we were hoarse. On Monday an officer finally came with our papers: 'I apologize. You were handed in here by mistake.' That was the only explanation. One day more or less in prison, what difference did it make? I could have boxed his ears. The camp where our soldier should have handed us over was about twenty minutes' walk away from this prison. Behind the barbed-wire gate a group of approximately fifteen men looked inquisitively in our direction. They were prisoners, it is true, but they no longer had close-cropped skulls. They looked clean and well fed, quite a contrast to the earlier days of 1948. I was suddenly shy. We had not seen a man for such a long time.

'It's Miss Goldacker, isn't it?'

'Yes, that's me. But excuse me, I don't think I know you.'

'Can you still remember the camp in 1946? You were working in the washhouse at the time, and one Sunday you brought me a pair of pants. You had stolen them for me. And before that you gave me the sheet of paper with the Paul Gerhardt words on it from the hymn book; you had brought the piece of paper with you from the Berlin prison. Both these gifts helped me so much.'

'Yes, of course, now I remember you!'

We looked at each other and smiled, and suddenly had nothing more to say. It was the Austrian baron who had been arrested by the Gestapo in Vienna and had then been 'liberated' by the Soviets. As he was still alive, the Soviets suspected him of carrying on working for the Gestapo even after the end of the war. I had had similar charges made against me.

When I had first met the baron, he had been more dead than alive: starved, half frozen, in despair. It was no wonder that I had not recognized him again.

Quite soon after my return home to Berlin I went to Vienna. I wanted to see my friends there, and, as I had his address, I took the opportunity to call there. An elderly lady, apparently his mother, opened the door when I rang. She kept me at the door and regretted that her son was not at home. My Jewish name and my North German accent were enough. I did not belong to her world.

In this Potma camp, the last one, everything was different; instead of gruel in the morning we were given coffee and bread and jam, at any time we chose. No longer was there a wake-up call. If people wanted to work, they could volunteer for kitchen duties, the only work still being done. Soldiers and officers treated us with almost friendly politeness. True, there was the roll call every day, just as there had been for the last ten years, but how friendly it all was now! In the morning a soldier would knock on the door of the hut before gently opening it: 'May I come in?' he would ask, one could almost have thought shyly.

'Yes, of course.'

'Can you tell me how many there are here in the hut, I don't want to disturb you.'

'Counting is your job, not mine.'

'Oh, I'll leave it then, I don't want my footsteps to wake people who are still asleep.'

Did they really believe that by means of this sickening friendliness they could undo ten years of suffering, ten years of hunger, ten years of cold and ten years of forced labour? Had they forgotten the legion of the dead?

There were wonderful summer days! In a little meadow behind my hut I could lie undisturbed in the sun throughout the day. What an almost forgotten pleasure! After the evening meal the canteen was available to us for all kinds of social activities; there was dancing almost every day. Where then were the ten years that lay behind us? Now and again we were shown a film, or else we sang. The men had set up football teams. We looked on and encouraged one or other of the teams with our cheers. In this way the period of waiting passed by.

One morning I was summoned to the man in charge of the camp. 'What will you do if we do let you go back to Germany?'

'I shall start where I left off when you arrested me: I shall finish my training as a teacher.'

'I see. But you are surely accustomed to earning your money in easier ways than that.'

'Do you think so?'

A few days later this game of question and answer was continued: 'Who apart from yourself has been involved in your case?'

'Nobody. I was sentenced on my own'.

'What is more, you even seem to be proud of it'.

Indeed I was proud. In Berlin, how often had they asked me the names of agents and collaborators during the nocturnal interrogations. How long had I kept silent? Until the day when I came out of the punishment cell and was able to give them a whole sequence of names, names of dead people whom I had known and whose personal description presented me with no difficulties while I was being cross-examined; I was sure that I would not make any mistakes.

I was proud that nobody was arrested because of me, and of how different I was. Rarely could my fellow prisoners claim this, as I learned during my captivity.

Finally the stage was reached when we were to 'hold ourselves in readiness' for the transportation. As one of the first, I stood just behind the gateway, with Ivan's black wooden case beside me. The well-known ritual began; an officer with a long list in his hand called out the names of prisoners in turn, and the prisoners went one by one through the great gate house. Outside soldiers were waiting. My name had been called out the previous evening. It was on the list. The officer had perhaps only left it out as he was calling out the others beginning with 'G'. I would come at the end. He did not call out my name. They went off without me.

The next day I was summoned again to see the camp officer. The interrogation continued. I had already understood the first time what they were after; they hoped by means of these interviews to persuade me to offer to work for them after my release. Through chance, without initiative on my part, I had become a 'political' prisoner. Without doubt they were now thinking of turning me into a real 'political'.

There were the same questions posed during the first interrogation: 'What are you going to do in Germany?'

'I've told you already, and I will repeat it again: I shall begin my life at the place where I was compelled to give it up; I shall take up my training to be a teacher again.'

Every time it was the same game of cat and mouse.

Once more a transportation was arranged, and once more I stayed behind alone behind the barbed wire; my wooden suitcase in front of me. Sonia was visibly pleased, her face beaming when she saw me coming slowly back to the hut. Her name had not yet been called.

I was intensely irritated. If my name were called out again, should I really be going?

Then one day we were both standing in front of the gate, both Sonia and I. At last! We were leaving Potma. Were we really going to Germany? No, not yet. But at least we were travelling in a train, in a compartment with other passengers; it was no longer a goods train, a cattle truck.

During the journey we had to change trains. We were standing on the platform of a small station, with brand-new wadded jackets, which we had received specially for the journey, hung casually over our shoulders.

Some Russians – free people – approached us in the hope of doing some bartering with us. Our new jackets attracted their attention, as did our new clothes! And suits! They had taken our measurements in Potma and then made the dungarees and full-skirted summer dresses out of light, voile-like material. The people were chased away by our guards; even so one of us attracted the attention of the soldiers, while the others made use of the opportunity and sold their state property to free Russian citizens.

Finally we arrived at Bikova, near Moscow, and were taken to a dasha where General Paulus was said to have been kept prisoner. The number of wadded jackets handed out to us no longer tallied, but two or three were still available, and we handed them to each other for them to be shown to the guard on duty. The house was too small to accommodate all the prisoners so a giant tent had been put up in the garden and opposite the house was a hut where Sonia and I had our quarters.

Now we were 'free' captives; we were getting good food, and nobody needed to work any more. I went for walks in the park, or read or played chess outside in the sunshine. This time of leisure was good for me; I looked plump and suntanned.

Then they summoned me to be interrogated again: 'What are you going to do in Germany?'

The same old story.

'In the first place I shall tell people that there's still no sugar to be had here, in the country that has won the war, ten years after it ended!'

Next day the prisoners who did our daily shopping in Bikova – naturally, in the company of a civilian – returned with mountains of sugar.

Then Sonia became ill, seriously ill. She was so weak that she could hardly speak. Nobody knew what was wrong with her, and the illness came so suddenly; no doctor was to be found. I sat at her bedside, she asked me to say the Lord's Prayer with her. I did so tearfully. I stayed with her, holding her hand, the whole night through. Her breathing was difficult, her pulse irregular, and still no doctor! How could I help her? No, she should not die; she should not be allowed to die, so close to the goal. That would be too unjust!

I had what seemed to me a wonderful idea; a nip of cognac would surely help her. I opened our common locker to take out the bottle which we had acquired in exchange for our wadded jackets at the little station where we had had to change trains, and which we had intended to save for the long journey to Germany. The bottle was there – empty! Only Sonia and I knew the hiding place. And I had held Sonia's hand, prayed with her and been fearful on her account, while all the time she had been dead drunk and I had not noticed anything. She had told me once that she had been an alcoholic before her imprisonment.

No, surely not! The interrogations were starting again.

'The Americans are ready and waiting to receive you straight away in the West.'

Now they were making themselves plain. So did I: 'If you believe that I am going to work for any government, you've made a big mistake; I shan't work either for the German government or for the Soviets or for the Americans. I've had enough!'

'We don't need your collaboration at all,' came the mocking reply, 'we have sufficient volunteers at our disposal who are most eager to work for us.'

Next day I was standing behind the gate with my black wooden case, summoned to depart. And I went through the gate to the other side – to liberty. If only I had had the courage to say what I thought earlier, I would have been in Germany much sooner.

A bus, not a lorry, was standing outside. We were driven through Moscow and shown all the sights like tourists. What trouble they were taking with us, as though they wanted us to be sorry to be leaving this beautiful city!

We came to the White Russian Station. We were not accompanied by a uniformed soldier; an officer in civilian clothes received us. We were only a small group, eleven men, Sonia and I. Actually we no longer looked like prisoners at all. In our made-to-measure garments we did not differ from the people who were hurrying along this way and that. Neither did my black wooden case attract attention; everyone in Moscow had cases like that.

We kept close to our officer. We were afraid that we might lose him in the crowd on the station at the last minute. What would happen to us without him? We had neither papers nor money.

The train was waiting at the platform. It was the Blue Express: Moscow – Brest-Litovsk – Berlin. Berlin – I could hardly move. I could only see the word 'Berlin'.

We got into the carriage which the officer had indicated discreetly to us by a slight movement of his head. Sonia and I were in a compartment on our own. I opened the window and looked on to the platform. It was a platform as on any station. People were embracing and kissing as they took leave of each other, while others were running alongside the train looking for seats. Passengers were looking out of the windows, just as I was doing. We were like them all, like the others – almost like the others. No one could tell from my appearance that I had no money and no passport. No one knew that I had ten years' forced labour behind me. We looked as they all looked. Slowly the train started moving. I looked at the big station clock; it was 14.23.

It was Wednesday, 24 August 1955.

The train got up speed. Our officer in civilian clothes counted us unobtrusively. Then he showed us how to change our seats into beds. Later he summoned us to a meal in the restaurant car. Dripping with sweat, we ate with knives and forks for the first time for more than ten years, and we felt awkward. But the next day we belonged to the people of this world.

This time we did not need to change trains at Brest-Litovsk. We only had a rather longer wait; the coaches were lifted and the gauge of the rails was changed. Nobody took any notice of us. The officer saw to the passport formalities, as discreet as he had been all along. We were going through Poland.

'Sonia, do you see the apple tree over there? An apple tree laden with ripe apples!'

Sonia and I fell into each other's arms. Some of the passengers who like us were standing in the corridor looked at us with surprise. The officer appeared and signified to us that we should return to our compartment.

'Sonia, you are crying.'

'You have tears in your eyes as well.'

Apples! We had forgotten in the ten years that there were such things as apples.

During the night the train stopped for a long time on the open track. In the distance we saw the lights of Warsaw.

At seven o'clock in the morning we were at Frankfurt an der Oder. Two uniformed members of the People's Police were waiting for us. One of them shouted to us! 'Form a line, in pairs!'

We laughed at him loudly and mockingly. Nobody thought of obeying his order. The Russian officer, still as discreet as he had been during the whole journey, turned away shrugging his shoulders and went off without saying a word. We, a disorderly crowd, got into a bus which took us to 45 Trebuser Strasse, Fürstenwalde. Once again we were in a camp. As we quickly found out, it was a reception centre for refugees from the west. Huts again, and still barbed wire. Our wanderings had not yet ceased.

A people's policeman took me to the office of the camp administration.

'Where are you going to from here?'

'To West Berlin, to my mother.'

'Exact address, please.'

I gave him my mother's address.

'Your mother is no longer living there. She has moved to East Berlin in the meantime.'

And he quoted an East Berlin address to me.

'Impossible. She would have told me that she was going to move on one of her last cards to me. All her cards came from West Berlin.'

'Show me one of the cards.'

'You know very well that I have no such card; we were not allowed to take any written material out of Russia: neither cards, letters nor books.'

'That is very convenient for you, isn't it?'

I asked him to telephone Berlin or to send my mother a telegram. The people's policeman answered me with an ironic smile: 'That is impossible. You must decide where you want to go to, to East Berlin or to West Berlin. But I warn you: if you cannot find your mother in West Berlin, the way back to East Berlin is a difficult one! So which address do you want to give? Think it over carefully!'

There was nothing to think over. During my ten years' imprisonment I had had ample opportunity of getting to know these people and their methods. I repeated the West Berlin address.

A delivery van brought us clothes from an East German department store: skirts, jackets, blouses, suits, shoes and stockings. What unwonted elegance! We could choose for ourselves. I chose a loose-fitting, bright green jacket, a black, wrap-around skirt, a white blouse and black plastic shoes. My black wooden case was overflowing. I had to keep it together with thick twine.

The camp office gave me a piece of paper, a little white sheet with a green strip across it. It was a police notification of departure from 45 Trebuser Strasse, Fürstenwalde. Not a word about where I had worked, starved and suffered for the last ten years of my life. As if nothing had happened – a notification of departure.

Then they gave us a railway ticket to Berlin and five marks in East German money.

Four of us had said that we wished to go to West Berlin. The gate was opened; we went to the station without supervision. For the first time for years there was nobody in front of us and nobody behind us. This was also something I had to get used to. In the train we tried to behave as unobtrusively as possible. Here, in East Germany, my wooden case would attract attention.

We had to leave the train at Erkner and travel on by the City Railway. The people's policeman who was keeping watch on the platform made difficulties for us, and would not accept our little white notifications of departure as credentials. The other passengers showed their identity cards and were let through. In the end another people's policeman made a telephone call and at last we were allowed through the barrier. Because of this delay we missed the connection to Berlin. We had more than half an hour to wait. At a kiosk we bought Berlin pancakes and a glass of cognac with our East German money. We did not speak to one another.

When the train came in and eventually stopped, we got in very quickly. We were all at once in a great hurry. Friedrichshagen, Köpenick, Lichtenberg – where I had worked at Aceta, where I had spent months in prison, where I had been sentenced and from where, more than ten years earlier, I had been deported to Russia.

I changed at Ostkreuz, mechanically, as I had always done in the old days. Three more stops and I would have to get out and continue my journey by tram. The train was still waiting. A loudspeaker announced, twice in succession, that we were now leaving East Berlin. I looked round. Nobody seemed to pay any attention to what we had just heard; nobody noticed me and my wooden case.

I cannot remember how I got out at the next stop. I only know that down the stairs in the station hall I had to lean against the wall; but I soon recovered myself. I had to continue by tram. How was I to pay for the ticket? I had no West German money. I turned to the man at the newspaper kiosk, and said: 'I've just come from Russia. Can you please give me ten pfennigs for the tram? I'll let you have it back tomorrow. '

'Don't make me laugh! Anybody can come along and say they've just come from Russia. I never lend anything to anybody. Is that clear?'

That was my welcome in my home country.

Opposite the station a policeman was standing. I hated uniforms. Nevertheless I went up to him and asked him for ten pfennigs, He laughed good humouredly: 'Ten pfennigs? You won't get anywhere for that. Ten years ago, yes, it would have been possible, but now a tram journey costs at least three times as much.'

'Very likely. But then it is quite ten years since I last went by tram. I've just come from Moscow.'

He looked at me closely, noticed my wooden case and understood.

'Listen, little lady, if you've been over there for ten years, they must have given you something on paper before they released you. Isn't that so?'

I showed him my white paper with the green strip across.

'Well, see now, that's it. Show this paper to the tram conductor. That will be enough.'

I boarded the next tram, and my white paper really was enough. I placed myself in a corner at the back and turned my face to the window. Nobody saw my tears. In the places where there had been ruins at the end of the war, big buildings had sprung up. A great many things looked different and yet there were many things which I recognized.

How often had I dreamt of this moment up there in the Arctic Circle. Then, whenever I woke up, I realized that it could never be anything but a dream – but now I knew I was not dreaming.

At every stop the conductor called out the name of the street. The nearer we came to our road, the more rigid I became, as if paralysed. When we reached the stop, I got out as if I were sleepwalking. I went across the road. It was very hot, and the wooden case got heavier and heavier. My mother was seventy years old. Would she stand up to the shock of seeing me again? When I had last been able to write to her – it was from Bikova – it was to say that she was not to expect me before Christmas, and today was 27 August 1955.

I reached my road without meeting anybody. It was the middle of the day. The ruins had disappeared; my road, which had been so badly damaged by bombing, had been reconstructed exactly as it had been before, just as I had seen it a hundred times in my dreams. I could hardly go on.

There I was in front of our garden gate; I went up the narrow path leading to our little house and saw my mother. She was sitting in the forecourt beneath the vine arbour and her back was turned to me. Her sister, my Aunt Elisabeth, was sitting facing her; she rose slowly and came towards me.

'Is that the postman?' my mother asked and turned round towards me.

'Emmy,' was all that she could say. And then: 'Come, let's go inside, let's have a look at you, child!'

My aunt was set on giving me something to eat; they were eating their dessert, chocolate blancmange with vanilla sauce. How could I eat? I saw my mother's face through a veil. There were ten years between us.

By five o'clock in the afternoon the whole family was there. We sat beneath the vine-covered canopy, and my aunt was staunchly bringing us things to eat. She had been busy all the afternoon making preparations, although no doubt she would gladly have sat in the garden with the rest of us. My large family were around me. How rich I was! It was Saturday and in the evening the church bells were ringing.

The next day I went to church. As we came away, a woman who was standing by the church door looked at me with large, luminous eyes, seized my hand and called to everyone, whether they wanted to hear it or not: 'Here she is, brought back by our prayers. For ten years we have been praying for her safe return.'

The first week was difficult. In the first place I had to find myself. Then I had to prove that I really was myself in all the places where my mother had informed people that I was missing. Shortly after my arrest my mother had been taken into custody for a short time – twenty-seven hours – and during this time our Britz house had been searched. In the course of this search all my papers had been taken away – my birth certificate, various testimonials and other papers. They had never been returned. At the police station, not far from the school from which I had been taken ten years before, I had to come with two witnesses who swore on oath that I was in fact Emmy Goldacker.

In Neukölln town hall I found myself facing the man who had denounced me. In the meantime he had become a duly appointed official. He could have been my murderer. He turned crimson when he recognized me. I turned to his colleague. I saw in my mind's eye a scene that I had witnessed in Britz shortly after the end of the war; two former concentration-camp prisoners were hanging a woman in the open street. She had denounced them to the Nazis. There must be an end to it all some time. I was alive. Was that not enough?

In another office of the town hall I asked permission to start again at the point where I had had to stop because of my arrest: I asked for a grant so that I could continue my interrupted training as a teacher.

'But you are a secretary, so you have training, don't you? Try to find work in your former profession. We don't have grants for people like you.'

Cold as ice.

After many difficulties I was at last given papers. The only thing that was still missing was my birth certificate. As I had been born in the East, I had written to inquire if they would send me a copy of the document. From the East came in reply the suggestion that I should come over in person to collect it. Naturally I did not do this; I could manage to live my life very well even without a birth certificate.

At first my mother went everywhere with me. I was afraid of the big city, afraid of people. I often saw the same man behind me, again and again. For my own reassurance I bought myself a tear-gas pistol which I always carried around with me.

The 'American Research Institute' took an interest in me and the years I had spent in Russia. 'The Soviets were not wrong, after all,' I thought.

Then there came a letter from East Berlin. As I had not been in Berlin for such a long time, it was proposed that I might like to be shown East Berlin. The rendezvous, Café Warsaw.

I did not respond to either of these approaches.

My only childhood friend invited me to visit her in England. On 31 December 1955, New Year's Eve, I sailed on a freight steamer from Hamburg across the North Sea to Hull. There were only a few passengers on board. I went on deck. It was a stormy night; the moon came and went from behind fluffy clouds; high waves broke against the bow of the ship. I was alone on deck – and this time I was free.

The next morning I arrived at my friend's home in Hull. Later on, at the home of my friend's mother, I met a young English teacher who had very recently come back from Istanbul. Her husband, a Rumanian journalist, knew Serge and told me that he had been married since the autumn of 1948 and now lived in Bucharest and was working for the Soviets.

'I have connections and can get a letter to him without it going through the censor. Why don't you write to him?'

'No,' I replied, without a second thought.

The wooden suitcase, given to me by Ivan Ivanovich, was put in the cellar of my mother's house. It should have remained there. But, when I looked for it years later, I could not find it. The refugees from East Germany staying with us had used it as firewood.

Chéserex, 14 July 1979

EPILOGUE

In 1955, with ten years of imprisonment in a labour camp behind me, I was in Moscow for the first time, impatiently waiting to be released. One day, I had to go out with one of the guards, both of us dressed in civilian clothes. He showed me the sights of Moscow including, of course, Red Square, the Kremlin and in front of it the famous store, GUM, where I was to spend the last of the roubles I had earned in the labour camp. (I was not allowed to take money out of Russia.) I bought a smart pen and pencil set. Trying out my new pen, I wrote my name in Cyrillic letters on a piece of white paper, proud of my achievement.

In 1992, I was in Moscow for the second time but with my husband, Fred. We were two of twelve people travelling with a Swiss guide. We arrived in Moscow in the evening and immediately took the underground to Red Square. There we were, where I had once been in 1955 as a prisoner, but now my husband was next to me. It was as if I were paralysed; I hardly dared to breathe, afraid to break the spell. But no, it was true, we were standing in Red Square like many other tourists, quite normal people. I almost shouted out loud with sudden, joyful laughter and felt deep gratitude.

Early next morning we left Moscow and took a flight to Tomsk, a town which up to then even Russians could visit only with a special permit. The next day, a boat took us along the Tom and the Ob to a lost village on the Tom's hilly shores. We left the boat and hurried as fast as we could up through the dense undergrowth of a steep hill. Grey clouds covered the sky and it rained just a little. I didn't mind the rain and made my way to the top of the hill breathing the keen, fresh air of September. I reached the village and walked further ahead till I reached the very end of the hill. An old, long-abandoned, wooden church stood at the end of the path. I was transfixed once more by this endless landscape which had long ago imprinted itself on my memory when I was a prisoner. We were not far from the old church and just gazed further and further into the distance. I remembered the hay harvest, when a canal boat had taken us slowly along the Pechora during the night so that we could find more grass the next day somewhere else in the tundra. And I remembered how the fine rain fell on me as I travelled on the boat not knowing where I would be in a year's time. My sentence had been nearly completed. Where would I be? The future had seemed dark and uncertain. A year later I was in Berlin, then England and finally Switzerland where I found work at the Ecumenical Institute not far from Geneva. I married and after years of a full and rich life, there I was again in Russia, glad to be there together with Fred.

On the way back through the village there was an old woman staring at us from behind her fence. I stopped, wanting to offer her some soap and chocolates. She hesitated but finally could not resist these treasures. She took them gratefully and asked me to wait a minute. Off she went and disappeared into her small hut. Coming back, she offered me a bunch of carrots and seeds from her garden flowers. Her sparkling eyes illuminated her old, wrinkled face. That's how I know Russia; that is my Russia. Once back in Switzerland we planted the seeds in our garden and ate the carrots which were delicious.

We hurried down the hill to get back to the boat. While we had been visiting the old, wooden church and the village, those who had stayed on the boat had prepared a delicious, cold meal for the rest of us. There was salted fish, sauerkraut, tomatoes and even caviar, salmon, champagne and vodka. Once more, I felt that life was just marvellous.

That evening, Fred and I left our guesthouse to post some cards. On the way we asked an elderly woman where to find a letter box which she showed us willingly. I thanked her and gave her some needles. She accepted with great pleasure and immediately took one of the needles and gently pricked or 'stitched' our hands: that was how she prevented bad luck for all of us. If she hadn't done that, who knows what might have happened? So, be careful before offering needles!

The next day and half of the following night we travelled by train from Tomsk to Omsk where we visited an art gallery and a museum and went on a boat trip on the Irtych, that vast Siberian river. As we embarked, we were greeted by such loud American music that we had to shout to make ourselves understood. Was Russia already losing its identity?

After another night in Moscow, the aeroplane brought us back to Zürich. We waited for the next train to Lausanne with a young man from our group who showed us a new guide to Russia which he had bought before leaving Moscow. 'You are mentioned in this guide,' he said and opened the book at page 411. It was true. There was my name and *Der Holzkoffer* under 'Recommended literature'. I still have no idea who recommended my book and put my name into this guide.

In 2005, Fred and I were invited to Moscow to launch the Russian edition of *The Wooden Suitcase.* Perm, St Petersburg and Moscow were the cities scheduled for conferences and readings. The Russians received us in state – admittedly without a red carpet, but that was about the only thing missing. Again we were surrounded by marvellous, human warmth and cordiality. At our hosts' (my translator Natalia Palagina's and her husband Sasha's) home, steaming borscht was waiting for us, prepared by Sasha.

Next morning the reading trip began. The organization was perfect. For the first time I realised that Natalia Palagina was not only an excellent translator but also an efficient manager. Receptions, organization – all of it gave me tremendous satisfaction. More than that, it gave me happiness. Former political prisoner 0-320 presented her book in Perm, a city once surrounded by prison camps.

We went to St Petersburg, and then back to Moscow.

In Moscow the reading took place at MEMORIAL, an organization trying to find and to rehabilitate former political prisoners, and to inform their families. Minutes before the beginning of the conference, someone from MEMORIAL came up to me and said there was something he had to tell me.

'A few days ago, when I was at the Moscow War Prisoners' Archive, I came across three letters in your file addressed to you in August 1955. If you give us permission to access these letters, we could photocopy them and send the copies to you.'

Three letters, letters written to me half a century ago. I instantly thought of my mother. Tears were welling up. I suppressed them and agreed to the gentleman's suggestion. Letters from my mother, letters from the dead, I was thinking, but, right then, I had to give my speech.

In November 2005, I received photocopies: of a letter from my mother, written on 19 August 1955 – a letter from a mother who had been waiting for my return for ten years. She died 22 years ago, here at our home in Switzerland.

The second letter was from old friends in the camp. They were feeling sorry for me because I had to celebrate my 36th birthday on my own, without them. All three of them have died, meanwhile. But who wrote the third letter?

It was a letter signed by me, but the text above the Cyrillic signature was obviously not mine. It was addressed and written to the General Secretary of the Communist Party, Mr Khrushchev, in person. Prisoner Goldacker, Emmy Pavlova, whose term expired several months ago, and who, furthermore, knows that there is permission for her release to West Germany, herewith politely asks Mr Khrushchev for her release to be included in the next repatriation transport to West Germany, scheduled for 10 August 1955.

I do not know of any prisoner ever having been so well informed! This alone proves that the text of this letter, dated 5 August 1955, and signed by me, was written by one of my guards. But who could have written it? Perhaps the man in civilian dress who had to show us the sights of Moscow and who was with me when I tried out my new fountain pen in GUM, by writing my name in Cyrillic letters on a piece of paper? This will remain a mystery, forever.

Emmy Goldacker, Cheseaux, 21 March 2006

APPENDIX:

Text of Emmy Goldacker's sentence*

File № 00232
SENTENCE

In the name of the Union of Soviet Socialist Republics
On 25 September 1945, the military tribunal of the Berlin garrison consisting of the presiding Major of Justice [name removed], and members of Red Army [name removed], with the secretary Lieutenant [name removed], and with the participation of [name removed], in a closed judicial session in Berlin, examined the case against German subject Goldacker Emma, born in 1919, native of the city of Dessau, federal state of Anhalt, Germany, who has a secondary education, white-collar worker, not a member of any party, unmarried, in the crime provided for in Art. 58-2 of the criminal code of the RSFSR [Russian Soviet Federated Socialist Republic].

With the materials of a preliminary and judicial investigation, the military tribunal established:

The defendant Goldacker Emma, from 1942 until April 1945, was a collaborator for the administration for national security of the German 'SD' [Sicherheitsdienst], fulfilled the duties of agent – radio operator and agent – messenger in the German consulate of Turkey, and the agent of Germany with the Japanese consulate in Hungary.

Working in the sixth division of the 'SD', Goldacker performed work on the registration of agents from amongst a number of Soviet prisoners of war, recruited by Germans, dispatched to the territory of the Soviet Union. She thus helped German authorities to perform work against the Soviet Union.

On the basis of the above mentioned, the military tribunal found Goldacker Emma guilty of the crime provided for in Art. 58-2 of the criminal code of the RSFSR, being guided by Art.319-320 of the

* Translation from the Russian provided by Emmy Goldacker, who received this from Russia in 2010.

155

Criminal and Procedural law of the RSFSR sentenced:

Goldacker Emma, on the basis of Art. 58-2 of the criminal code of the RSFSR, to be subjected to deprivation of freedom and held in reformatory camps for the period of ten years. The period of Goldacker's punishment starts from July 1945. The sentence is final and is not subject to cassation appeal.

Presiding [signature]

Members [two signatures]

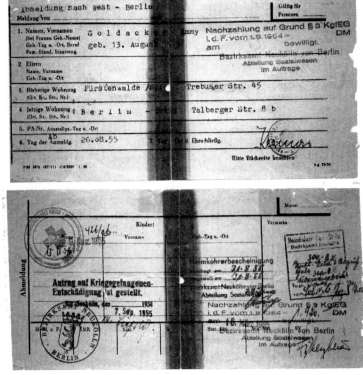

Emmy's ID card after her release from the prison camp, 1955